METAPHYSICS
AND THE
IDEA OF GOD

WOLFHART PANNENBERG

Translated by Philip Clayton

WILLIAM B. EERDMANS PUBLISHING COMPANY
GRAND RAPIDS, MICHIGAN

Originally published as *Metaphysik und Gottesgedanke,*
© 1988 by Vandenhoeck & Ruprecht, Göttingen

Copyright © 1990 by Wm. B. Eerdmans Publishing Co.,
255 Jefferson Ave. S.E., Grand Rapids, MI 49503

Printed in the United States of America

Library of Congress Cataloging-in-Publication Data

Pannenberg, Wolfhart, 1928–
[Metaphysik und Gottesgedanke. English]
Metaphysics and the idea of God / Wolfhart Pannenberg;
translated by Philip Clayton.
p.   cm.
Translation of: Metaphysik und Gottesgedanke.
Includes bibliographical references.
ISBN 0-8028-3681-X
1. God. 2. Philosophical theology. 3. Metaphysics. I. Title.
BT102.P31513   1990
211—dc20   90-30878
CIP

CONTENTS

TRANSLATOR'S PREFACE

"THE CONNECTION between being and time makes it possible to forge a much closer connection between philosophical reflection and the biblical experience of reality" (p. 109). With these words Pannenberg summarizes a central theme of his *Metaphysics and the Idea of God*. His project over the last three decades has been to fight against the ghettoization of theology and to demonstrate "the convergence of philosophy and religion." In the present book, the dialogue partner is the metaphysical tradition, a discipline especially well suited for clarifying, or challenging, theology's concept of God. The following pages offer, I believe, an excellent introduction to the crisscrossings of theology and metaphysics over the last two thousand years, as well as a sophisticated analysis of the problems and opportunities that the metaphysical tradition presents to the theologian today.

The English version of *Metaphysik und Gottesgedanke* consists of two parts. Part One, "The Idea of God," contains five lectures on metaphysics presented in Naples in 1986. Part Two, "Metaphysics and Theology," contains Pannenberg's critique of process theology (published as an appendix to the German edition) and two additional essays that bear directly on the questions addressed in Part One.

One might argue that this was a book that Pannenberg had to write. English-speaking readers have for decades been demanding a fuller development of his controversial "eschatological ontology," a fuller explanation of claims such as, "it is necessary to say that, in a restricted but important sense, God does not yet exist."[1] Closer to home, Pannenberg had been urged by philosophers at the University of Munich (including Dieter Henrich and Lorenz Puntel) either to lay his metaphysical cards on the table or to cease claiming metaphysical justification. Perhaps Pannenberg's ontology "does need to be thought through in an exercise at least as elaborate as Whitehead's *Process and Reality*," and perhaps we need "a new philosophy of time."[2] But it now seems unlikely that Pannenberg will work out an "ontology of anticipation" in such detail. Presumably he would maintain that the present volume—like his earlier books on christology, philosophy of science, and anthropology[3]—at least clears the ground sufficiently for the three-volume *Systematic Theology*, the first volume of which is currently being translated for publication by Eerdmans. In any event, these eight essays also stand on their own as contributions to the ongoing debate on the concept of God within metaphysics.

The reader will notice here the strongly historical orientation of much of Pannenberg's earlier work. Each chapter contains its own metaphysical thesis; yet Pannenberg explores each thesis in the light of the central debates of the

1. Wolfhart Pannenberg, *Theology and the Kingdom of God* (Philadelphia: Westminster, 1969), p. 56.

2. Allan Galloway, *Wolfhart Pannenberg* (London: George Allen & Unwin, 1973), p. 97.

3. Respectively, see Wolfhart Pannenberg, *Jesus—God and Man*, 2nd ed., trans. Lewis Wilkins and Duane Priebe (Philadelphia: Westminster, 1977); idem, *Theology and the Philosophy of Science*, trans. Francis McDonagh (Philadelphia: Westminster, 1976); idem, *Anthropology in Theological Perspective*, trans. Matthew O'Connell (Philadelphia: Westminster, 1985).

Western philosophical tradition. Frequently, the treatments begin with a modern challenge to metaphysics (Kant, Feuerbach, Heidegger), gradually moving backward through time to classical themes and responses. The book is thus addressed to philosophers who are concerned with the critique of religion in purely philosophical terms. But it can also be read as a general introduction to metaphysical reflection on God, somewhat on the order of Colin Brown's *Philosophy and the Christian Faith* or Diogenes Allen's *Philosophy for Theologians.*[4]

In chapter 1, Pannenberg grants that Heidegger's case against metaphysics would mean abandoning the concept of God required by Christian theology. But Heidegger's proclamation of the end of metaphysics presupposes the ultimacy of the question of Being, as well as the difference between *Being* in general and individual *beings*. Pannenberg attempts to render these presuppositions suspect in order to defend a continuing place for the question of God within metaphysics. Chapter 2 reviews the modern debate about the nature of the Absolute, focusing on Schleiermacher, Descartes, and Kant. Pannenberg argues that the (allegedly unsolved) tensions in Kant's *Critique of Pure Reason* leave the door open for pre-Kantian theories of the Absolute. In particular, arguments from Descartes, later developed by Hegel, for the primacy of the Infinite remain central for elucidating a metaphysically adequate doctrine of God.

After Kant, many philosophers turned to self-consciousness as a new basis for metaphysical reflection. In chapter 3, Pannenberg argues that self-consciousness cannot be used to explain its own genesis. Hence we are justified in turning to a theory of the Absolute to provide a context for understanding human development. At the same time, Pannenberg grants that Feuerbach's critique of God as a human

---

4. Colin Brown, *Philosophy and the Christian Faith* (Downers Grove, IL: InterVarsity, 1968); Diogenes Allen, *Philosophy for Theologians* (Philadelphia: John Knox, 1985).

projection reveals a serious problem with such strategies: as long as we work backward from the existence of subjectivity, trying to uncover the Absolute at its source, we remain liable to the suspicion of creating the Absolute as "only an emasculated mirror image of self-consciousness" (p. 62). Metaphysicians therefore need to establish a broader explanatory framework, encompassing both subjectivity and world, in order to validate the concept of the Absolute.

The problem of time forms a constant backdrop for these essays. Chapter 4 interacts again with Heidegger's position, insisting that his existential, individualistic perspective is inadequate to bring being and time together. A consideration of various alternatives leads finally to Plotinus. Preferable to Augustine, Plotinus defends eternity as the whole which precedes and is the source of time. Every temporal present thus presupposes and anticipates a final completion of time. This definition sets the stage for chapter 5, in which Pannenberg offers a metaphysical defense of his now-famous tenets: a future (eschatological) ontology and an objective (anticipatory) theory of meaning. The future is active in the present through anticipation and is the necessary condition for meaning, judgment, assertion, truth.

Each of the three essays in Part Two deals in some way with the need for metaphysics and theology to be holistic, to work at the level of the broadest possible framework. Chapter 6 challenges the adequacy of Whitehead's atomism, arguing that process thinkers need to supplement Whitehead's metaphysics with the holism of thinkers such as Bergson, Alexander, and James. Chapter 7 examines the categories of "part" and "whole" in more general terms, challenging philosophers such as Hegel who subordinate these categories to other philosophical frameworks. Finally, chapter 8 defends the centrality of the experience of meaning for evaluating religious truth claims, outlining an "objective" theory of meaning that is dependent on the outcome of history as a whole.

These eight essays do not claim to present a complete doctrine of God; they are meant to complement Pannenberg's Systematic Theology and other earlier treatments of these themes.[5] The chief task of these chapters is to create a coherent synthesis out of the central considerations—religious *and* philosophical—that have fueled metaphysical reflection on God. This "reading together" of two (often arbitrarily isolated) traditions into a single defense of the idea of God represents the book's thesis and, if successful, its most impressive achievement.

*　　　*　　　*

In general, I have taken very few liberties with the original text. Paragraphs and sentences have, of course, been freely subdivided. In seeking to make Pannenberg accessible to a broader audience, I have often used multiple synonyms to help convey the sense of obscure German terms. I have included the German [in brackets] only in the case of important technical terms or when a paraphrase of the original was necessary. Finally, where the German referent was only implicit (e.g., constructions with *davon, daraus, dagegen*), I have sometimes taken the liberty of making the reference explicit.

Rendering Pannenberg into readable English is not a one-person task. Dustin Anderson and Jonathan Bolton have read large portions of the manuscript, making extensive criticisms and suggestions for improvement; they deserve much of the credit for whatever readability the translation

---

5. See Pannenberg, *Systematische Theologie*, vol. 1 (Göttingen: Vandenhoeck & Ruprecht, 1988), esp. chaps. 2, 5, and 6. Important recent secondary works include Stanley J. Grenz, *Reason for Hope: The Systematic Theology of Wolfhart Pannenberg* (New York: Oxford University Press, 1990); Carl Braaten and Philip Clayton, eds., *The Theology of Wolfhart Pannenberg: Twelve American Critiques* (Minneapolis: Augsburg, 1988).

may finally have attained. I have consulted with my Williams colleagues Daniel O'Connor and Alan White on technical questions in medieval philosophy and German Idealism.

Finally, I would like to acknowledge that earlier versions of the chapters in Part Two appeared in other publications (though, in two cases, in abridged form). Chapter 6 below is a revision of a translation by John C. Robertson, Jr., and Gérard Vallée, and chapters 7 and 8 are revisions of my own translations.[6] I thank the publishers for their kindness in permitting me to use this material.

PHILIP CLAYTON

6. Chapter 6 appeared originally as "Atom, Duration, Form: Difficulties with Process Philosophy," *Process Studies* 14/1 (Spring 1984): 21-30. Chapter 7 was first published as "The Significance of 'Part' and 'Whole' for the Epistemology of Theology," *Journal of Religion* 66 (Oct. 1986): 369-85. Chapter 8 was originally published as "Meaning, Religion and the Question of God," in *Knowing Religiously*, ed. Leroy S. Rouner (Notre Dame: University of Notre Dame Press, 1985), pp. 153-65. We gratefully acknowledge permission to use this material.

PREFACE

IN RECENT YEARS we have heard from many sides that it is
necessary to return to metaphysics—the field of study once
taken to be "first philosophy"—as the object of our intellectual attention. It cannot be a matter of indifference to theology
when philosophers again take upon themselves these themes
that have been neglected for so long. Christian theology is
dependent upon the conversation with philosophy, especially for the clarification of its discourse about God, but also
for its work on the relationship between God and created
reality. Moreover, theologians have repeatedly made their
own contributions to the development of philosophical
thought within the history of metaphysics.

The reflections published in this volume go back to a
series of lectures given in April 1986 at the Istituto Italiano per
gli Studi Filosofici in Naples, to which I had been invited in
May 1983 at the conference on "Hegel's Logic of Philosophy"
on the island of Capri. The challenge to pull together into a
single context some of my reflections concerning philosophy
gave me the opportunity to bring into explicit focus those
connections with philosophical themes which in my earlier
publications had remained peripheral or had been dealt with
only implicitly. My comments could now start out from the

state of the discussion within philosophy. Nonetheless, even here the treatment has remained necessarily fragmentary.

I would like to thank the young Italian philosophers who took part in the course in Naples for their intensive discussions and for a wide variety of criticisms, which have led to clarifications in the reworked version of the lectures and in the notes that follow. More than anything else, the discussions in Naples compelled me to flesh out my originally somewhat sketchy treatment of consciousness and subjectivity into a chapter on its own (chap. 3), which now follows the chapter on the idea of the Absolute. By contrast, the criticism of process philosophy, which I presented in Naples in connection with the introduction, has now been moved to Part Two, which also includes, in the English edition, revised translations of two previously published articles on related themes. I view process philosophy as this century's most significant contribution to metaphysics. But the goal of that particular chapter is nonetheless more critical than systematic, whereas, in the five chapters of Part One, critical comments stand in the service of a systematic intention which runs through all five chapters. The path which this systematic intention takes will hopefully stand out more clearly with the present ordering of the chapters.

For clarity concerning the thoughts developed in this volume, I am grateful for intensive conversations with Dieter Henrich—more so than can be seen from the few references to him in the text—and especially for the seminars which we held together in Munich on the topic "Theology and Metaphysics." More than anything else I thank Dieter Henrich and my Italian friends, especially Valerio Verra, for the encouragement to take up, once again, the continuing dialogue between philosophy and theology.

I would like to express my thanks to my assistant, Christine Axt, for her help in correcting page proofs.

Munich, December 1987   WOLFHART PANNENBERG

PART ONE

THE IDEA OF GOD

CHAPTER 1

THE END OF METAPHYSICS
AND THE IDEA OF GOD

THE VIEWPOINT that has become dominant over the last two centuries holds that the age of metaphysics has come to an end. On this question we find agreement between rather diverse thinkers: on the one side, Auguste Comte, the founder of positivism, along with his modern disciples, especially within the twentieth-century school of analytic philosophy known as "logical positivism"; and on the other, Friedrich Nietzsche, along with the philosophers of Neo-Kantianism, as well as Wilhelm Dilthey and Martin Heidegger. For all of these thinkers, the concept *metaphysics* characterizes a particular (and long-drawn-out) phase of the history of humanity; and all understand themselves to be thinkers of a postmetaphysical age. We will have to explore whether there is agreement among these thinkers on the various views of metaphysics and of its demise, as well as their understandings of the postmetaphysical situation in the present.

Since the time of Albrecht Ritschl (1881), even Christian theology has closed itself off from metaphysics; indeed, theology has even worked programmatically to purify itself from the various metaphysical influences that the so-called Hellenization of Christianity had on the Christian doctrines

3

of God, world, and humanity. Since Adolf von Harnack's *History of Dogma*, the educated Christian community has viewed the Hellenization of Christianity as an estrangement from the original, simple gospel of Jesus. For the moment we can ignore the question whether Harnack really meant his criticism to be read in this way. At any rate, many theologians have seen it as their task to free the Christian experience of faith from the encrustations that had been built up by metaphysical thought and had taken a firm hold on the dogmas of the Church.

In recent years, a growing number of voices have been calling for a renewal of metaphysics. Of course, there were always outsiders within philosophy who carried forward the tradition of metaphysical thought. These figures included English Hegelians at the beginning of this century; a large number of those philosophers who stood close to the Catholic understanding of faith; individual thinkers such as Nicolai Hartmann in Germany and, more recently, Wolfgang Cramer; and finally, the process philosophers Samuel Alexander in England and Alfred North Whitehead and Charles Hartshorne in the United States. Among these various efforts, process philosophy deserves particular attention; I will thus treat it on its own in chapter 6 below. The influence of process philosophy, especially in American theology, has again grown after the ebbing of the high tide of logical positivism and the ordinary language philosophy stemming from the later Wittgenstein.

Significantly, the demand that we again concern ourselves with metaphysical themes which were once vehemently opposed has even been heard from the middle of the linguistic-analytic camp itself, namely, from Peter Strawson at Oxford—even if his call is only for a *descriptive metaphysics*, a reflection on the implications of our awareness of experience. Similarly, I find it noteworthy that in the center of the transcendental-philosophical tradition of German philosophy, one finds Dieter Henrich maintaining that there is "no successful life . . . without metaphysics."[1] For this reason, Henrich claims, the ultimate questions must once again be raised. In making this claim, Henrich goes much further than Strawson. For him, these questions involve more than spelling out the implications of our empirical knowledge. They also imply a knowledge that is to be acquired via a "counter-move" [*Gegenzug*] to the empirical consciousness, which is derived from the basic relationship between the ego and the world. What necessitates the countermove, according to Henrich, is a certain opacity [*Dunkelheit*] of the forms of experience, one which is unavoidable as long as we remain at the level of natural consciousness.

In theology as well, the rejection of metaphysics cannot be successful over the long haul. In Catholic theology, of course, the attempt to supply a metaphysical foundation for theology was never really abandoned, only modernized. This occurred especially through the so-called transcendental Thomism of Maréchal, Rahner, Lotz, and Coreth. These thinkers attempted an anthropological or transcendental-philosophical interpretation of Scholastic (especially Thomistic) philosophy and a corresponding rethinking of metaphysics and the philosophy of religion. With their assertions concerning the ontological state of humanity, world, and God, these Catholic thinkers certainly overstepped the boundaries of strict transcendental reflection in the Kantian sense, which is capable of speaking only of the conditions of possible experience as they are found within the experiencing subject. Consequently, either the results of their work must be cast into doubt in principle, or their methods of transcendental reflection must be transformed into another mode of reflection.

Within Protestant theology during the first half of this century, especially Paul Tillich and Karl Barth (although in rather different directions) formulated statements about God, humanity, and the world that are possible only given

---

1. Dieter Henrich, *Fluchtlinien* (Frankfurt: Suhrkamp, 1982), p. 23.

the presuppositions of metaphysics. Nonetheless, neither Barth nor Tillich reflected methodologically on this fact, because they developed their reflections as an interpretation of the Christian experience of faith. In Tillich, for example, one can recognize connections with Schelling's later philosophy, connections that seem still to form the basis for Tillich's own later writings. Yet in his *Systematic Theology* he did not mention these influences. The truth claim of such self-affirmations of faith, as one encounters them in Barth or Tillich, is nonetheless not independent of the question whether their metaphysical assumptions can be conceptually justified. If they cannot, then the theological self-interpretation of faith can only express the subjective commitment of the theologian.

More than anything else, theological discourse about God requires a relationship to metaphysical reflection if its claim to truth is to be valid. For talk of God is dependent on a concept of the world, which can be established only through metaphysical reflection. Christian theology must therefore wish for and welcome the fact that philosophy should begin, once again, to take its great metaphysical tradition seriously as a task for contemporary thought. Unfortunately, theologians today rarely concede this dependence upon metaphysics. Nevertheless, the dependence is only too clear: a theological doctrine of God that lacks metaphysics as its discussion partner falls into either a kerygmatic subjectivism or a thoroughgoing demythologization—and frequently into both at the same time!

A renewed concern with metaphysics is unlikely to take place unless one challenges the arguments upon which the thesis of "the end of metaphysics" is based. The meaning of this thesis is certainly not the same for all of its adherents. According to positivism, for example, we see in human history first the replacement of the rule of religion and mythical thought by the rule of metaphysics, and this in turn by the authority of the empirical sciences. Even in this century this thesis was advanced by the logical positivists of the Vienna Circle. Thus Ludwig Wittgenstein in 1920 and Rudolf Carnap in 1928 acknowledged only those statements to be meaningful which could be empirically verified or were of a purely logical-analytic nature. Since statements about God are in principle not empirically verifiable—at any rate, not during the epoch of modern natural science—they are not only false but are from the outset meaningless as assertions.

As it turns out, logical positivism was not able to sustain its strict criterion of meaningfulness. According to the criterion, many other statements, such as the assertion of laws within natural science, will fall under its verdict of meaninglessness. Moreover, the verification principle itself cannot be verified. Consequently, A. J. Ayer realized already in 1946 that the verification principle could only be defended in such a weak form that even metaphysical sentences could no longer be declared unworthy of rational discussion and hence excluded. Moreover, the demand of the later Wittgenstein that we trace the philosophical use of language back to its everyday context did not lead to the dissolution of metaphysics, though many attempts in this direction were made, notably those of Gilbert Ryle in England and, more recently, Ernst Tugendhat in Germany. Interestingly, the idea of God has withstood such attempts with particular persistence.

The thesis of the end of metaphysics developed by Wilhelm Dilthey in *An Introduction to the Human Studies* (1883) stands in marked contrast to positivism's thesis. The difference is already clear from the fact that it is not natural scientific reflection but ultimately historical reflection which, according to Dilthey, brings the epoch of metaphysics to an end. For Dilthey, the mistake of metaphysics lies in its failure to recognize the relativity of the forms taken by the human spirit. Metaphysics is "logicism," as represented for Dilthey most clearly by Hegel's system. Dilthey characterized the "assertion of a seamless logical context" in everything that happens by means of the Principle of Sufficient Reason as "the logical root of every consistent metaphysics." However, the "feeling of life" in humans and the "content or understanding of the world given to humans" cannot "be exhausted within the logical context of a universally valid science." For Dilthey this insight is the outcome of historicism. Consequently, his concept of metaphysics and of its end was a very different one from that of the positivists, for whom it was precisely the universally valid science which brought about the end of metaphysics.

Heidegger's position stands remarkably close to that of Dilthey, in fact closer to it than to Nietzsche's view. Nietzsche understood "the end of metaphysics" to mean that the Platonic doctrine of two worlds—the assumption that there is a hidden world behind the world of experience—had become untenable. By contrast, Heidegger and Dilthey are linked together in their view of the relationship between metaphysics and logic. In his article on the onto-theo-logical constitution of metaphysics, Heidegger maintains that metaphysics has "logic as its principal and pervasive trait," corresponding to the Leibnizian Principle of Sufficient Reason.[2] Heidegger attributed this domination of the attempt to "ground" all thought within metaphysics to the understanding of "Being" as "Ground," a view that goes back to the doctrine of Logos in Heraclitus.[3] According to him, the logical character of metaphysical thought also provides the explanation of "how God comes into philosophy," namely, as "the grounding Ground" of the totality of all that is.[4] This is why he claimed that metaphysics is not only onto-logic but onto-theo-logic.

---

2. Martin Heidegger, *Identity and Difference*, trans. Joan Stambaugh (New York: Harper & Row, 1969), p. 70. German edition: *Identität und Differenz* (Pfullingen: Günther Neske, 1957). [Page references are to the English text; in some cases I have altered the translation.—TRANS.]

3. Ibid., pp. 57-58; cf. pp. 54-55.

4. Ibid., pp. 58-59.

It was precisely against this theological essence of meta-physics that Heidegger now turned his criticism: as long as the metaphysician separates the Being of beings as "Ground" from Being as the most general principle, the essential unity of metaphysics eludes us; it remains "unthought."[5] Put differ-ently: the difference between Being and beings is not appro-priately conceived when the Being of beings is conceived as Ground.[6] For, according to Heidegger, the very distinction between the Ground and what grounds it is already de-pendent upon the difference between a being and Being. If one takes the "step back" from the metaphysical form of thought[7]—if one stands at a distance from the whole history of metaphysics—then one can see that the view of Being as the most general principle is inappropriate.[8] Equally inappro-priate, according to Heidegger, is the claim that metaphysics as ontology must necessarily be theology. The latter claim Heidegger called "rash," because it would be valid only under the presupposition of the domination of the Logos.[9] As a result, Heidegger maintained, "someone who has experi-enced theology—that of the Christian faith as well as that of philosophy—out of the heritage in which it grew, will today prefer, in the realm of thought, to remain silent concerning God."[10] For the onto-theological character of metaphysics has allegedly become "questionable" because of "experiencing a [way of] thinking to which has been shown the still *unthought* unity of the essence of metaphysics in onto-theo-logy."[11]

According to Heidegger, philosophy should cease to speak of God, because metaphysical discourse about God is

---

5. Ibid., p. 60.
6. Ibid., pp. 70-71.
7. For example, ibid., p. 52.
8. Ibid., pp. 66-67; cf. p. 51.
9. Ibid., pp. 55, 59ff.
10. Ibid., pp. 54-55.
11. Ibid., p. 55.

constrained by the difference between Ground and what is grounded, while, however, leaving this constraint itself unthought. Yet Heidegger believes that silence about God in the realm of thought corresponds to the Christian faith. As he sees it, when faced with the God of metaphysics, the *causa sui*, humans can "neither pray nor can they make offering to him. Before the *causa sui*, they can neither fall on their knees in awe, nor can they make music and dance before this God."[12] In his writing on "Phenomenology and Theology" from the years 1927 and 1928, Heidegger stressed that theology is at any rate not a "speculative knowledge of God," but rather a science of faith in the sense of a "mode of existence of an individual human being."[13] Indeed, faith is a mode of existing that stands over against philosophy's form of existence as its "mortal enemy," because faith transcends and eliminates pre-faith existence as such.[14]

It is thus clear that Heidegger, unlike the tradition of the Middle Ages, does not view theology as the "science of God," but rather as reflection on faith. Therefore, theology should "avoid the application of any sort of philosophical system."[15] Faith, for its part, he treats only as a product of existing. Hence, for Heidegger, there can be no talk of an object of faith that might precede the act of faith: "Revelation is not the transmission of items of knowledge."[16]

By advocating this interpretation of theology, Heidegger may have found himself in agreement with Rudolf Bultmann, but he stood in sharp opposition to theological tradition and, in the theology of his time, to Karl Barth. Without a doubt, the Christian proclamation of the cross and resurrec-

---

12. Ibid., p. 72.
13. Martin Heidegger, *Phänomenologie und Theologie* (Frankfurt: Klostermann, 1970), pp. 25, 18.
14. Ibid., pp. 32, 29.
15. Ibid., p. 24.
16. Ibid., pp. 18-19.

tion of Jesus of Nazareth meant to convey the knowledge of a particular occurrence. Christian faith knows itself to be grounded upon this, its object. It was in this sense that Paul wrote to the Romans: "If you confess with your lips that Jesus is Lord and believe in your heart that God raised him from the dead, you will be saved" (Rom. 10:9). The object of Christian faith precedes it historically. For precisely this reason, according to Augustine, Christian faith is dependent upon authority, since the historical realm for the ancients was accessible only through authoritative guarantees. But to the objects of faith that precede the act of faith belongs—in the first place and above all else—the reality of God. For this reason the missionary proclamation of the early Church attempted above all to turn people to faith in the one God (1 Thess. 1:10; Heb. 6:1). Turning to the one God was the foundation for the second theme of the early Church's message, namely, the proclamation of Jesus, whom God had raised from the dead, as the "Son" of God who will come again and who "delivers us from the wrath to come" (1 Thess. 1:10).

In proclaiming the one God, Christianity appealed almost from the start to philosophy and to its criticism of the polytheistic beliefs of other peoples. The reference was first to the Stoic theories and later, above all, to the doctrine of God found in Platonism. Such an appeal to the philosophical doctrine of God must not be interpreted only in an external sense as an accommodation to the spiritual climate of Hellenism. Instead, it reflects the condition for the possibility that non-Jews, without becoming Jews, might come to believe in the God of Israel as the one God of all humanity. The appeal to the philosophers' teachings concerning the one God was the condition for the emergence of a Gentile church at all. We must therefore conclude that the connection between Christian faith and Hellenistic thought in general—and the connection between the God of the Bible and the God of the philosophers in particular—does not represent a foreign in-

11

filtration into the original Christian message, but rather belongs to its very foundations.

Corresponding to the fundamental significance which the message of the one God has for the Christian mission is the fact that the focal point for Christian theology lay from the very beginning in the doctrine of God. Christian theology, in contrast to Heidegger's construal of it, is essentially an inquiry [*Wissenschaft*] into God and his revelation. Everything else that occurs within theology can become a theme for the theologian only "in relation to God," as Thomas Aquinas put it: *sub ratione Dei.* Christian theology would lose not only its specific content but also, and most importantly, the consciousness of truth that is intrinsic to it, if it were to follow Heidegger's advice to stop speaking of God in the realm of thought.

And how do things stand with philosophy? In *Identity and Difference* Heidegger had raised the question: "How does God come into philosophy?"[17] The question assumes that "God" does not already belong to the origins of philosophy itself. According to Heidegger, philosophical reflection means "freely and on one's own letting oneself enter in to what exists as such."[18] This definition has clear consequences for metaphysics: metaphysics is "theo-logic because it is onto-logic."[19] If one grants to Heidegger the priority of the theme of Being, then it becomes understandable that he could ask, How does God come into philosophy?

But of course Heidegger knew that, viewed historically, "God" was a theme within philosophy from the very beginning, namely, in the question of the ultimate beginning, the *prōtē archē.*[20] "As long as we search through the history of philosophy merely historically, we will find throughout that

---

17. Heidegger, *Identity and Difference,* p. 59.
18. Ibid., pp. 56-57.
19. Ibid., p. 60.
20. Ibid.

God has come into it."[21] Put more precisely: God—namely, the God and the gods of religion—already precedes the origins of philosophy, and philosophical inquiry is from the very beginning a *return inquiry* [*Rückfrage*] concerning the gods of religion, concerning the *theologia* of the poets, as Plato put it. In its beginnings, philosophy was a return inquiry concerning the actual or true form of the divine. Werner Jaeger clearly established this point in *Die Theologie der frühen griechischen Denker* [The Theology of the Early Greek Thinkers], and the fact has been further corroborated since then through a large number of individual studies, particularly through the work of Uvo Hölscher. The philosophical return inquiry has sought to conceptualize the divine from the outset as a unitary entity, corresponding to the unity of the cosmos. This is the common element in the critical attacks of the Ionic philosophy of nature upon the religious tradition.

Thus even Heidegger acknowledged that, viewed historically, God has always already been within philosophy. Nonetheless, he continued: "But assuming that philosophy, as thinking, is freely and on one's own letting oneself enter in to what exists as such, then God can come into philosophy only insofar as philosophy, of its own accord and by its own nature, requires and determines that and how God should enter into it."[22] But what are we to make of this "But assuming"? What kind of assumption is it, and on what grounds is it justified? How is this assumption related to the "step back" that Heidegger wanted to accomplish?

Perhaps, if philosophy is taken to be an inquiry into what exists as such, then the philosopher does step back in some sense from the history of metaphysics and, in particular, from its origins. But the ground on which the philosopher treads in taking this step has itself a place within the history of philosophy. Which place is that? Parmenides may have

---

21. Ibid., pp. 55-56.
22. Ibid., p. 56.

already taken Being as the ultimate object of philosophy, a position that was impressively strengthened by the Eleatic Stranger in Plato's dialogue, the *Sophist*. Still, it was Aristotle who first explicitly raised the question of Being, of what is as such. Heidegger then declared the Aristotelian question of Being to be the ground of philosophy in general, turning this supposition against its deeply rooted origins in the question concerning the true form of the divine. But in so doing, Heidegger opened himself up to the question whether his own thought paid sufficient attention to the mediation of the question of Being through the question of God.

It is, then, not true that God can find a place in philosophy only to the extent that "philosophy, of its own accord and by its own nature, requires and determines that and how God should enter into it." In the first place, such a claim contradicts the idea of God in a rather crass fashion, in that it must be unacceptable to the divinity of God that some other court of appeal should determine the manner in which he enters into human reflection. Moreover, philosophy as an essentially historical discipline is not as set apart, as independent from all determining conditions, as Heidegger represents it. Hegel wrote with greater accuracy when he said that philosophy has always stood historically in relationship with religion, bringing to conceptual expression [*auf den Begriff*] the truth that had already appeared in religion.

Of course, philosophy does not play this role without raising critical reservations about the religious tradition. Since religion speaks of God and gods whose power is expressed within the world, it includes claims concerning the reality of the world; hence philosophy is justified in appealing to experiences in the world in order to raise criticisms of the religious tradition. When philosophy takes on the role of critic, philosophical thought does stand on its own, as Hegel has shown. But when it does so, philosophical reflection not only opposes the claims of the religious tradition—it also (and primarily) confronts *every* form of consciousness that limits itself to perceptions of finite objects encountered in our experience of the world. As Dieter Henrich writes, philosophy corresponds to the deeply rooted human need to come up with interpretations of life that run counter to the orientation of the so-called natural consciousness, which focuses on the objects that belong to our experience in the world.[23]

If this is true, philosophy converges with religion— the various philosophical criticisms of religion notwithstanding. For religious experience and theological reflection also run counter to the type of consciousness that limits itself to experiences of finite things and to interaction with them. So it was that Schleiermacher accused "understanding and practical persons" of suppressing and suffocating the meaning [Sinn] of the universe even in their children. His opponents "fetter humans to the finite, indeed to an extremely small portion of it, . . . in order that the Infinite should be kept as far as possible from their eyes."[24]

The convergence of philosophy and religion, both of which are opposed to the everyday awareness of experience with its orientation toward finite things, enables theologians to use philosophy as they seek to bring the awareness of God within religion to conceptual expression. Such use of philosophy has perhaps been most fully developed within Christianity. Now religion, philosophy, and theology need not become amalgamated as a result. In religious consciousness, the divine reality normally stands in the center and insists upon its priority over against all other forms of consciousness; and matters are similar within theology. By contrast, within philosophy the

---

23. Henrich, *Fluchtlinien*, pp. 17-18.

24. Friedrich Schleiermacher, *On Religion: Speeches to its Cultured Despisers*, trans. Richard Crouter (Cambridge: Cambridge University Press, 1988), p. 146. German edition: *Über die Religion. Reden an die Gebildeten unter ihren Verächtern*, Philosophische Bibliothek, vol. 255 (Hamburg: Felix Meiner, 1958), p. 80 (1st ed. p. 144). [Page references to the German edition will be given in parentheses. —TRANS.]

main focus is on justifying one's opposition to the natural consciousness and on moving away from the experience of life that is based on it. As a result, philosophers stress the requalifying of the objects that we encounter in our consciousness of the world, rethinking them from the perspective that is achieved by going beyond the finite givenness of the world.

Only by "rising above" [*Überstieg*] (D. Henrich) finite objects and above the ego to which they are given can we bring the "world" as their essence into view. "World" here means the whole within which each individual object receives its place. But note that the concept of world emerges within the religions only *along with* the concept of the divine in which the whole of the world is grounded. In short, the theme of the Absolute or of the one God of philosophy has a role in our understanding of the world and whatever subjectivity corresponds to the concept of world, and this theme is encountered whenever we rise above the multiplicity of givens that we experience within the world.

But of course philosophy, like theology, can also concentrate on the theme of the Absolute in such a manner that it seeks to conceive it as the condition of the finite itself and thus as prior to all finite reality. This focus on the Absolute means interpreting the finite as merely the product of the self-differentiation of the Absolute. For example, we find such a use of philosophy in Spinoza or Hegel. But even in these cases some sort of path to the standpoint of absolute knowledge must be provided. Hegel suggested one such path in the *Phenomenology of Spirit,* another later in the Introduction to his philosophical *Encyclopedia* and in the treatment of the various standpoints of thought toward objectivity which he calls an anticipation [*Vorbegriff*] of the encyclopedic logic.

Consequently, we cannot simply decide in advance whether, as Heidegger says, it is appropriate for philosophy today to cease speaking about God within the realm of thought. The question must be approached by carrying out the philosophical countermove to the everyday understanding of the world and the self, and by this "rising above" toward the absolute One. Only by engaging in philosophical reflection will we be able to tell whether the concept of God can be made sufficiently comprehensible on the basis of finite human subjectivity and as its product. If it cannot, it will then be clear that we must move beyond even this subjectivity through philosophical reflection, that only reaching the end of the ascent in the absolute One can provide the basis for an adequate interpretation of the experiences of the divine within the various religions.

In taking on this task, we will have to provide a detailed assessment of the arguments of postulated atheism, that is, the approaches that postulate the nonexistence of God in order to preserve the freedom of human subjectivity. In contrast to these views, Heidegger's defense of his claim that we must be silent concerning God within the realm of thought has significantly less merit, for it rests completely on his judgment regarding the fundamental place of the question of Being and, in particular, on the difference between Being and beings. But this claim of Heidegger's should be approached with serious reservations.

I suggest that the theme of the One—understood as the goal of the ascent above the multiplicity of what is given in the consciousness of worldly objects and one's own ego—is philosophically more fundamental than the distinction between beings and Being.[25] We can trace this tendency toward

---

25. This claim need not imply that "the One" is the highest concept of the Absolute. It has at first to do only with the theme of the metaphysical ascent above the multiplicity of finite things. The formulation of the ascent theme using the concept of the One is more comprehensive than viewing it in terms of origins, which is only one of the forms of the metaphysical question concerning the One. The absolute One can be thematized not only as the source but also as the completion of things. Further, the One is the condition of the multiplicity itself, since every multiplicity is composed of elements, each of which is a one. The concept of the One thus encompasses the theme of the metaphysics of

the One all the way back to the attempts to identify the one
archē in the very beginnings of Greek philosophy. By contrast,
Heidegger's declaration that the question of "what is as
such" is *the* theme of philosophy seems rather artificial, especially when one considers that he distanced himself from the
Aristotelian conception of Being as what is most general.
Only in its function as the most general—and thus as the
expression for the One which encompasses everything—
could "what is as such" become for Aristotle the theme of
foundational or first philosophy. More basic within Greek
thought was the question of the true nature of what is, in
contrast to what is transitory. Yet this question too was from
the very beginning bound up with the concept of the One in
contrast to the many. Although the devaluation of the transitory was acknowledged already in antiquity (and even more
in modern thought!) as needing criticism, the question concerning the One remains unavoidable.

We have now reached an issue that is of far-reaching
significance for the relationship between philosophy and
religion: Can the metaphysical ascent toward the concept of
the One fully grasp the reality of the Absolute on the basis
of independent philosophical reflection, and can it sufficiently establish its conclusions? Or is philosophy capable
only of formulating criteria which every conception of the
absolute One must satisfy, while being unable to grasp the
reality of the Absolute fully or to sufficiently justify its
acceptance? This is the problem that is associated with the
so-called proofs of the existence of God and with any philosophical theology that is based upon them. For, in the past,

---

the finite as well as the metaphysics of the Absolute. By contrast, it
remains an open question through what source each finite thing is one
in itself, and hence a something at all. In the same way, what constitutes
the unity of the Absolute also remains open. Even the formation of the
concept of the Absolute, in contrast to the finite, goes significantly
beyond that of the One in its determinateness.

whenever philosophy claimed to be in the position to derive the true conception of the one God and to be able to prove his existence through the power of philosophical reflection alone, one finds, bound up unavoidably with that belief, the claim to stand in the place of the revelation-based knowledge of religion.

I hold that such claims were exaggerated and have been justly criticized. The history of the proofs of the existence of God within modern thought, from Descartes through Kant and Hegel, shows the necessity of extending reason to include the idea of God. It does not show that the existence of God, prior to all human consciousness and to the existence of the world, can be proved. Bound up with this result is the fact that metaphysics has always had difficulties in conceiving the absolute One as personal and therefore as "God" at all. It could well be that the very possibility of speaking philosophically of "God"—that is, of ascending above the multiplicity of what is finitely given toward the absolute One and of linking this ascent together with the concept of God— remains tied to religion. Likewise, on the other side, the metaphysical "counter-project" [Gegenentwurf] to the everyday understanding of the world—an understanding that assumes a "fundamental relationship" between the ego and the world—has never been able completely to grasp "that which it takes its departure from."[26] The metaphysical "rising above"[27] remains bound to the immediacy of experience in the "fundamental relationship" among the ego, the world, and the Thou, and is unable to replace it. So also it seems to remain bound to the historically prior experience of religion, as is evident in the origins of philosophy in Greece as well as in India.

These limitations notwithstanding, the ascent to the absolute One can be effective as a critical corrective to the

26. Henrich, Fluchtlinien, pp. 17-18.
27. Ibid., p. 179.

images of the divine within the religious traditions. In fact, this corrective function may go so far in individual cases that basic elements in the traditions' understanding of God become untenable. This was the case in the relationship between Greek philosophical theology and the polytheistic view of the divine within the Greek religious tradition. We find an analogous situation, though in a slightly different sense, in the modern critique of the Christian-theistic concept of God. Of course, in this second case the criticism has had to do more with a particular theological interpretation of the Christian understanding of God, which itself had been formulated in the wake of the influence of classical philosophical theology.

These brief remarks on the problem of the proofs for the existence of God should at least indicate that a renewal of metaphysical reflection within philosophy cannot simply involve reintroducing the same positions and the same approach to the problems that preceded the turn away from metaphysical reflection in the first place. This applies also to the themes associated with the philosophical doctrine of God. The connection of metaphysical reflection and reconstruction to the finitude and historicity of our experience, which must remain its starting point, cannot be overcome but can only be clarified.

The same also holds true for the relationship between philosophy and religion. Whenever philosophy uses the label "God" for the absolute One—the goal of the metaphysical ascent above everyday experience—it already makes use of the language of religion. We need find no mistake in this usage. In the first place, philosophical reflection has been related from the outset to a religious awareness of the divine which preceded it historically. Moreover, there is a thematic unity between the absolute One of philosophy and the one God of the monotheistic religions. For this reason these religions were able to draw on the absolute One of philosophy for the interpretation of their understanding of God; conversely, the religious understanding of God can become a source of inspiration for progress in the philosophical clarification of the notion of the Absolute. Still, within philosophy explicit discourse about God belongs perhaps more appropriately to the philosophy of religion than to metaphysics—unless, of course, the metaphysics of the Absolute should itself turn out to be connected to the philosophy of religion.

CHAPTER 2

THE PROBLEM
OF THE ABSOLUTE

THERE IS no metaphysics without the idea of the unity of reality. And because the unity of the real, understood as world or *cosmos*, is a unity that consists in the order of the many (i.e., of many individual things), the unity of the world raises the question of a ground, a foundation, that is able to order the many and hold it together as a unity.

According to Kant, both—the unity of the world as well as the idea of a ground for its unity, which (as the unity of a plurality) must be different from the world—express the need of human reason to discover an unlimited unity in the manifold of experience. At the same time, he held that this need could not be fulfilled as an idea or mere ideal of reason. For in the reality of our experience, human understanding never comes to an end in its attempt to synthesize the multiplicity of experience.

With these conclusions, Kant ended his reflection on subjectivity as the locus of human knowledge and as the source of the self-delusions that are a part of it. However, he did not take the step to what Dieter Henrich has called the "third reflection" [*dritte Reflektiertheit*],[1] which has as its goal

---

1. Henrich, *Fluchtlinien*, p. 51.

to show that reason, when left on its own, can only be a source of delusion. For the possibility of attaining knowledge through reason presupposes a fundamental correspondence between reason and the reality toward which it is directed. Any attempt to set reason and self-subsisting reality against one another is then itself, as Hegel noticed, a product of reason, or rather of the understanding, and must lead to delusion if it is declared to be truth itself.

Our consciousness of experience has always both an objective and a subjective side: in it the unity, and the difference, of subjectivity and extrasubjective reality are always already present. The same structure holds for self-consciousness, as well as for the relationship between self- and object-consciousness. Something similar should then also hold for reflection on the totality of experienced reality. Admittedly, this totality is given only as a thought and not as knowledge, since it depends on the individual objects of possible experience that are bound together in it. No experience has in fact grasped and comprehended the totality of possible objects of experience. Nevertheless, the idea of the totality of all reality that could ever be experienced is more than an arbitrary subjective thought, since, in one form or another, this idea is the condition for grasping and determining all the individual objects of experience. We shall return to this theme below.

When we view the objects of possible experience from the objective side (rather than as subjectively constituted), we can characterize them, in the most general terms, as what exists; more precisely, as what exists finitely. For, as parts of the totality of such objects, they are always "something" in distinction to other such objects. To characterize objects in this general sense as what exists, and indeed as what exists finitely, makes it possible to conceive them in their variety as elements of a manifold, and thereby also as components of the totality of objects—however these objects may differ qualitatively from one another in other aspects.

The idea of the finite can be characterized both ontologically and noetically. We can understand the finite ontologically as implying a real ending in space and in time, as being limited by another; noetically, insofar as every "something" is what it is in its particularity only by being differentiated from an other. This demarcation of one thing from an other (or from all others) is what constitutes its *concept*. So, for example, the Greek word for border, *horos*, is at the same time the word for concept.

Yet, whenever we think of a border, we have always thought at the same time of a something that lies beyond that border, however vaguely. As Hegel showed convincingly in his *Logic*, we cannot think the border without thinking the other that lies on the far side of the border.[2] Now the other, in demarcation from which the finite is what it is, is either another finite thing or *the* other of the finite as such, that is, the

---

2. G. W. F. Hegel, *Hegel's Science of Logic*, trans. A. V. Miller (New York: Humanities Press, 1969), pp. 127-29. German edition: *Wissenschaft der Logik*, 2 vols., ed. George Lasson, Philosophische Bibliothek, vols. 56-57 (Hamburg: Felix Meiner, 1967), 1:113-16. [References to the German edition will be given in brackets.—TRANS.] However, Hegel does not claim that only our reflection (in that it borders "something" off from the other and thinks it by means of this bordering off) is at the same time beyond this border. He also ascribes such transcendence beyond its own finitude to the something itself (p. 128 [116]; cf. the comments on Limitation and the Ought, pp. 131ff. [119ff.]). The something could thus appear to him as the "beginning of the subject" (p. 115 [102]), namely, as "itself" relating to itself in its negation. But I cannot follow Hegel in this claim. In the forms of the "Logic of Being," the notion of negativity is not yet grasped as belonging to the forms themselves. As Hegel himself says, they are transformed [*eingehen*] into one another. It is not possible to speak of a self-movement in the case of the determinations of the "Logic of Being" in the sense that Hegel later claims concerning the Logic of the Concept. Correspondingly, the transition from the finite to the idea of the Infinite is not to be understood as an activity of the something but rather is carried out by the human understanding, even though the nature of the something gives rise to the transition.

Infinite. Both of these are suggested by the border that is contained within the very notion of the finite: the finite in its specificity suggests the other finite from which it is distinguished; and the finite as finite per se, in its generality, suggests the Infinite. The notion of the finite as such can therefore not be thought without already thinking the Infinite at the same time—at least by connotation, certainly not always explicitly. It is only by reflecting on the finitude of what is finite that we are led to the explicit thought of the Infinite.

That any adequate comprehension of the finite already implies the Infinite is the basic idea of Schleiermacher's theory of religion in the *Speeches:* "All that is finite exists only through the determination of its limits, which must, as it were, be 'cut out' from the Infinite."[3] But "understanding and practical persons"[4] do not perceive this; they interact with finite things as if they were what they are in and of themselves. Only at a higher stage of awareness do we perceive the dependence that lies in the very notion of the finite, the dependence of every finite object with regard to the "determination of its boundaries" (and therefore its definition) on the Infinite. Only then do we experience simultaneously the Infinite that lies within finite things and the finite that is its manifestation. This deeper consciousness of what the reality of finite objects is, according to Schleiermacher, constitutes the religious consciousness.

Note also that this insight—namely, that comprehending anything finite depends upon the intuition of the Infinite— was already expressed by Descartes at one important point in the third of his *Meditations.* There he attempts to show that the idea of God has been impressed upon the human spirit by nature itself. In making his point, Descartes appeals to the idea of the Infinite. This idea, he claims, is not merely a secondary construction of our thought, one that might be derived by

---

3. Schleiermacher, *On Religion*, p. 103 (30, 1st ed. p. 53).
4. Ibid., p. 146 (80, 1st ed. p. 144).

negation from the idea of the finite. Instead, the relationship is the opposite: "And I must not imagine that I do not conceive infinity as a real idea, but only through the negation of what is finite. . . . On the contrary, I see manifestly that there is more reality in infinite substance than in finite substance, and my notion of the infinite is somehow prior to that of the finite, that is, the notion of God is prior to that of myself."[5]

Descartes thus claims a priority of the idea of the Infinite over all other representations of our consciousness, because they all arise only through a process of limitation of the Infinite. He may have derived this conception from Heinrich of Gent, one of the greatest Scholastics of the thirteenth century. Furthermore, as Descartes explicitly admits, the same priority of the Infinite holds also with regard to the idea of the individual ego. Emmanuel Levinas has correctly noticed in this admission a reversal from the *cogito*, the point of departure for the *Meditations*. Although the *Meditations* set out from the certainty of the *cogito*, this certainty does not, after all, have its ground in itself, for the conception of the individual ego already presupposes that of the Infinite.

Descartes thus proceeded in a less subjective manner than one fashionable construal of the history of philosophy would have us believe. Only if we have already presupposed the idea of the ego as a given does the *cogito* yield the certainty which Descartes claimed for the starting point of his *Meditations*. He was able to proceed as he did because, in our actual state of consciousness when we begin to philosophize, self-consciousness is in fact presupposed. However, the idea of the ego is in no way given through itself, but rather presup-

---

5. René Descartes, *Discourse on Method and Meditations,* trans. Laurence Lafleur (Indianapolis: Bobbs-Merrill [Library of Liberal Arts], 1960), pp. 101-2. Latin edition: *Meditationes de prima philosophia,* 1st ed. (Paris, 1641 / Amsterdam, 1642), pp. 28-29 (*Med.* III, §§ 23-24); reprinted in *Meditationen über die erste Philosophie,* ed. Erich Chr. Schröder, Philosophische Bibliothek, vol. 250 (Hamburg: Felix Meiner, 1956), p. 78.

poses the idea of the Infinite. The ego itself results from a limitation of the Infinite, as do all other representations of the finite.

These insights notwithstanding, Descartes' argumentation remains problematic in two respects. First, Caterus already posed for Descartes the question of whether we actually have a "clear and distinct" idea of the Infinite. In his answer, Descartes praises it as an "intelligent question," while remarking that he took great pains to forestall this objection. And in fact, he writes in the passage cited above from the Third Meditation that the perception of the Infinite is "somehow" (quodammodo) prior to that of the finite. He explains this, in the answer to Caterus, as follows: The Infinite as such is "admittedly in no way grasped conceptually and yet nonetheless is understood." It can only be understood from the finite, namely, "in a negative fashion," although what we understand in the process is something "positive to the highest degree," which we nonetheless cannot adequately grasp. Rather, our comprehension is "just as when we turn our eyes to the ocean. Admittedly, our view does not cover the whole ocean, and we do not measure its infinite expanse. Yet still one says that we behold it."[6] Even with this illustration, however, Descartes has not adequately realized that the intuition of the Infinite, the intuition that precedes all finite representations, is not present as an explicit thought but only in an *unthematized* fashion within all representations of the finite. By contrast, the explicit treatment of the Infinite no longer precedes all finite subjects. In fact, it even presupposes the general notion of the finite, in that the thought of the Infinite, once thematized, does indeed take the form of a negation of the finite.

---

6. René Descartes, response to the first criticisms (by Caterus), in *The Philosophical Works of Descartes*, 2 vols., trans. Elizabeth Haldane and G. R. T. Ross (Cambridge: Cambridge University Press, 1967), 1:17 (= *Meditationes de prima philosophia*, 2nd ed. [Amsterdam, 1685], p. 149).

The second problem in Descartes's exposition lies in his much too rash identification of that "somehow" (*quodam-modo*), with which the consciousness of the Infinite precedes all other contents of consciousness, with the idea of God. Of course, such an identification is not only suggested by the traditional definition of God as infinite essence (*essentia infinita*), but is also argued for by Descartes: the Infinite has a greater degree of reality (and thus of perfection) than the finite, which can only be represented as a limitation of the Infinite: "I see manifestly that there is more reality in infinite substance than in finite substance." It is expressly this higher perfection of the Infinite "on account of which" (*proinde*) Descartes claims its priority over the experience of anything finite.

Here we encounter the concept of an All of reality (*omnitudo realitatis*), which Kant, in connection with Baumgarten, would later label an "ideal of pure reason." Each finite object can only be understood as a limitation of the *omnitudo realitatis*. Of course, Kant no longer discussed the derivation of this concept from the notion of the Infinite. I will have to return to this fact, for it exposes a major weakness in Kant's treatment of the idea of God within his critique of reason. But for now it is sufficient to raise the question: Has Descartes in fact shown that the priority of the notion of the Infinite in our consciousness is a consciousness of God, simply because highest perfection is inherent in the conception of the Infinite?

I am skeptical of the claim that with the notion of highest perfection we have already reached the idea of God. The idea of God, however construed, has a considerably higher specificity than is inherent in the general picture of a being with maximal perfection. For the idea of God cannot be separated from the elements of personality (however we are to understand it) and of a will (whatever form it takes). It follows that the notion of a highest perfection as such is not yet identical with the idea of God. Of course, if we have arrived at the idea of God (especially in its monotheistic version) on other grounds, and if we then form the conception of a being with maximal perfection—and if, in addition, we raise the question of whom we should affirm this highest perfection—then in such a case it must be clear that this attribute can be affirmed only of the one God. It is in this sense that we are to understand Anselm's thesis that God is the being "greater than which none greater can be conceived" *(quo maius cogitari nequit)*. This sentence does not *define* the idea of God but already presupposes it and *predicates* of it the highest perfection.

I do not mean to deny that the Infinite, conceived in its full sense, and the highest perfection are in fact identical with God and can only be identical with him, that is, can only be predicated truly of him. But the general, confused, and prethematic idea of the Infinite does not explicitly connote identity with God. Even reflection on *perfection*—an idea that is connoted by the concept of the Infinite when it is thematized as such—is not sufficient to derive the concept of God, unless the idea has been derived from another source, namely, from the religious tradition. Of course, given this concept, we can maintain correctly that Infinity and highest perfection befit only the one God. Hence we can also say that the confused intuition of the Infinite, which lies, prethematically, at the basis of all human consciousness, is already in truth a mode of the presence of God, even though in it God is not yet explicitly known as God.

In the eighteenth century, the priority of the Infinite over the finite was discussed especially in connection with the concept of space. In his correspondence with Leibniz concerning Newton's concept of absolute space, Samuel Clarke characterized space as the expression of the immeasurableness or immensity *(immensitas)* of God. While Leibniz understood space to be only a form of ordering and relating things to one another,[7] Clarke conceived of absolute space as the

---

7. *The Leibniz-Clarke Correspondence,* ed. H. G. Alexander (Manchester: Manchester University Press, 1956), pp. 25-26. German edition:

vacant form of the divine omnipresence. This infinite empty space already lies at the basis of all distinctions between parts of space in our representations: *"Infinite Space is one,* absolutely and *essentially indivisible."*[8] Divisions of space arise only through the existence of the finite in space. Descartes's view of the priority of the Infinite in comprehending the finite may have had some effect on this thesis; at least it finds therein an additional confirmation.

The theme of infinity, in connection with the discussion of space, continued to preoccupy Kant. In the dispute on the nature of space between Leibniz and Clarke (who represented Newton's position), Kant, after much hesitation and under the influence of Euler, finally declared himself for the concept of absolute space.[9] Nevertheless, he continued to hold onto Leibniz's thesis of the subjectivity of space. In the "Transcendental Aesthetic" of his *Critique of Pure Reason,* Kant appropriated Clarke's decisive argument against Leibniz as part of his third argument concerning space. Space "is essentially one; the manifold in it, and therefore the notion of spaces in general, depends solely on [introducing] limitations."[10] Space is therefore "an infinite given magnitude."[11]

Streitschriften zwischen Leibniz und Clarke, in *Die philosophischen Schriften von G. W. Leibniz,* ed. Carl J. Gerhardt (Berlin: Weidmann, 1890), 7:363, no. 4 (Leibniz's third paper). [References to the German edition will be given in parentheses.—TRANS.]

8. Ibid., p. 31 (368 no. 3).

9. Cf. Max Jammer, *Concepts of Space: The History of Theories of Space in Physics,* 2nd ed. (Cambridge: Harvard University Press, 1969), pp. 173ff. German edition: *Das Problem des Raumes: Die Entwicklung der Raumtheorien* (Darmstadt: Wissenschaftliche Buchgesellschaft, 1953), pp. 192ff.

10. Immanuel Kant, *Critique of Pure Reason,* trans. Newton Kemp Smith (New York: St. Martin's Press, 1965), A 25. German edition: *Kritik der reinen Vernunft,* in *Werke,* 6 vols., ed. W. Weischedel (Wiesbaden: Insel-Verlag, 1960). ["A" designates the first German edition, "B" the second.—TRANS.]

11. Kant, *Critique of Pure Reason,* B 39-40.

All divisions in it are secondary. Kant's thesis that space is a form of intuition depends upon the primacy of the whole of space over its parts.

Unfortunately, the connection of the infinity of space with philosophical theology—as an expression of the immeasurableness of God—simply was not thematized by Kant. If he had done so, Kant's "Transcendental Aesthetic," like Descartes's *Meditations*, would have had to employ the idea of God—or at least a rudimentary preliminary form of it—as the condition of all finite knowledge. The idea of God would then not have appeared only at the end of the "Transcendental Dialectic," as an ideal of pure reason that is tied to the completeness of the employment of the understanding, but already at the beginning of the "Transcendental Aesthetic." In this case, the concept of God would then be constitutive for reason, and this would of course have given a completely different character to the Kantian critique of reason as a whole. In particular, it would mean that the position of the critique could no longer be that of a transcendental subjectivity standing on its own; rather, in the intuition of the Infinite the opposition between subject and things-in-themselves would already be bridged over and held together. But instead, Kant indeed acknowledged the primacy of infinite space (and of infinite time) for all experience of finite objects, while robbing the acknowledgment of its theological implications. When it reaches the level of the ideal of pure reason in the *omnitudo realitatis*, Kant's critique of reason no longer makes it possible to recognize that we are still concerned with the same theme as in the case of space and time, namely, with the priority of the Infinite for comprehending anything finite.

Incidentally, Kant did not consistently hold to the priority of the Infinite even in the form utilized in the "Transcendental Aesthetic." This is clear in the section of the "Transcendental Analytic" on the "Axioms of Intuition."[12] Here he

---

12. Ibid., B 202-7.

writes that all intuitions, precisely because of their dependence on space and time, are extensive magnitudes, in which "the representation of the parts makes possible . . . the representation of the whole."[13] While according to the "Transcendental Aesthetic" the intuition of the infinite whole of space (and also, analogously, of time) first makes possible the comprehension of the individual therein, according to the "Transcendental Analytic" the representation of the parts *precedes* that of the whole. Indeed, this fact is now taken to be characteristic for all intuitions—even though in the "Transcendental Aesthetic" the character of space and time as intuitions had been founded precisely upon the primacy of the whole over the parts. As a result, the approach taken in the "Analytic" gives rise to questions of the completeness of the synthesis accomplished by the understanding,[14] a question which leads to the problems of the "Transcendental Dialectic." But is not the entire line of reasoning that Kant eventually followed already superseded by the priority of the whole over the comprehension of the parts which he grants in the "Transcendental Aesthetic"?

The tensions or breaks within the *Critique of Pure Reason* between the "Transcendental Analytic" and the "Transcendental Aesthetic" have long been acknowledged in the literature,[15] without any solution having been found. I review them here in such detail only in order to counter the criticism that returning to Descartes's thesis of the priority of the Infinite over every experience might involve falling below

---

13. Ibid., B 203.

14. A 326-27, 328; cf. also 411ff.

15. See Christopher B. Garnett, *The Kantian Philosophy of Space*, 2nd ed. (Port Washington, NY: Kennikat Press, [1939], 1965), esp. pp. 207- 35; Hans Vaihinger, *The Philosophy of Immanuel Kant* (New York: Garland Publishing, 1976). German edition of Vaihinger: *Kommentar zu Kants Kritik der reinen Vernunft*, ed. Raymund Schmidt (Stuttgart: Scientia Verlag Aalen, 1970), 2:228.

the level attained in Kant's critique of knowledge. We have seen exactly the opposite: at this point in the *Critique of Pure Reason* an unresolved dilemma remains, which precisely requires turning back to the pre-Kantian discussion—indeed, one which casts the entire position of transcendental subjectivism into a rather dubious light. By contrast, we have found reason for viewing our two conclusions—on the one hand, the priority of the infinite whole of space and time over all comprehension of finite entities and relationships; on the other, the so-called transcendental ideal of the *omnitudo realitatis* as the condition of all conceptual determination—as merely different aspects of the same theme. If this is correct, then we must grant to philosophical theology a much greater importance in the critique of reason than Kant was willing to ascribe to it.

The criticisms that I raised above concerning Descartes's interpretation of the feeling of the Infinite as the idea of God already make it understandable, at least in part, why Kant did not wish to link the infinity of space together with the themes of rational theology. That the Infinite as such should have to do with the idea of God simply cannot be taken for granted, as long as one limits oneself to the concept of the Infinite in itself. To make the connection we need another—and for Kant more specific—point of view. Beginning in 1763, Kant developed a preference for the term *all-sufficiency (ens a se)* over *the Infinite*, of which "one ordinarily makes use," as an expression for the divine perfection. The concept of the Infinite appeared to Kant as "in its actual meaning obviously mathematical"—not in the sense of the unlimited extendability of the number series, as in the Aristotelian *potentially infinite* (which Descartes labeled *indefinit* to distinguish it from the actually infinite), but rather in the sense that the Infinite "surpasses all possible numbers," while standing in a relationship of similarity to the series of numbers. Since such a similarity is unacceptable in the case of God, Kant abandoned the concept of the Infinite in rational theology as of 1763.[16] But one must question whether the intuition of space as an infinite given magnitude, as presented in the fourth argument concerning space in the "Transcendental Aesthetic" of 1787, is really consistent with the discussion of the concept of infinity of 1763. For in the earlier treatment, the infinity of space is again supposed to *precede* all numerical definition and distinction.

The concept of the actual Infinite has had a firm place in the Christian doctrine of God since Gregory of Nyssa. It was treated, in particular by Duns Scotus, as fundamental for the entire doctrine of God, namely, for the proof of the unity of God. The Infinite is one because it has no other outside itself; and since it also cannot be conceived as divided, the Infinite is identical with the One. As a result, the concept of the Infinite is perhaps the most significant example of a philosophical concept which, without already being an idea of God in the actual sense, still functions as a criterion for the appropriate formulation of theological assertions about God: whatever stands in contradiction to the notion of the infinity of God cannot be a component of a rationally demonstrable notion of the one God.

Fichte, for example, made good use of this criterion in the atheism dispute in opposing the idea of God as person. As a result, one had the (not unjustified) impression in 1798 that the idea of God had been dissolved—especially since Fichte had presented a similar criticism against the idea of God as substance. Nevertheless, the function of infinity as a standard and criterion for the doctrine of God remained untouched in the dispute surrounding Fichte's "atheism." Whoever wishes to defend the notion of the personality of God against Fichte's argumentation must demonstrate that this concept can be identified with the idea of divine infinity.

Admittedly, the idea of the Infinite can serve this func-

---

16. Kant, *Critique of Pure Reason*, A 186 (= *Kritik der reinen Vernunft*, ed. Weischedel, 1:727).

tion only if it can be clearly distinguished from mathematical infinity. This distinction is the most important result of the Hegelian treatment of the Infinite as the Absolute. Hegel did not treat the concept mathematically as Kant had, but rather presented it purely logically, utilizing its opposition to the concept of the finite,[17] as was already implicitly the case in Descartes's assertion of the logical priority of the Infinite over the finite. Treating the finite in the light of its dependence on an other resulted for Hegel in the demand that the truly Infinite must exclude all dependence on an other. When we think about it in this way, we conceive the truly Infinite as identical to the Absolute, which does not need any other for its Being. All-sufficiency (in Kant's sense) is therefore shown to be the true content of the concept of the Infinite. At the same time, this concept has been distinguished from that form of mathematical infinity which Hegel characterized as the "bad Infinite" [*das schlecht Unendliche*] in contrast to the truly Infinite.

---

17. Hegel, *Science of Logic*, pp. 116ff., 137ff. (1:103ff., 125ff.). The something is finite insofar as its differentness from the other as border is unique to it as "the immanent determination of the something itself" (p. 117; cf. 129-30 [104; cf. 116-17]). Since Hegel spoke of a self-relation of the something toward its border (see n. 2 above), he could then conceptualize the Infinite on the other side of the border based on the self-relation of the something itself. This required presenting the Infinite as the infinity of the something itself insofar as the something is unified with itself in its other (see Hegel, *Hegel's Logic, being Part One of the Encyclopaedia of the Philosophical Sciences,* trans. William Wallace [Oxford: Clarendon, 1975]. German edition: *Encyclopädie der philosophischen Wissenschaften im Grundrisse,* ed. Friedhelm Nicolin and Otto Poggeler, Philosophische Bibliothek, vol. 33 [Hamburg: Felix Meiner, 1975], § 95). This "being for itself" is not the "bad Infinite" (see *Science of Logic*, pp. 138ff. [1:127ff.]). Rather, it is the true Infinite throughout, not simply set over against the finite (pp. 143ff. [132ff.]), but also developed out of the concept of the finite. By contrast, the Infinite as the "definition of the Absolute" (p. 137 [125]) also grasps the finite from itself, yet in a different manner, since the Infinite is alone the Real (p. 149 [139]).

Hegel's logical analysis of the Infinite leads us yet one important step further. As long as the Infinite is thought of only in opposition to the finite, its essence remains limited through its opposition to the finite as its other—which is precisely what characterizes things that are finite. Any infinity that we conceive as only abstractly transcendent, as standing in opposition to the finite, is itself finite. In order truly to be conceived as infinite, the Infinite must not only be set in opposition to the finite but must at the same time overcome this opposition. It must be conceived both as *transcendent* in relation to the finite and as *immanent* to it. With this analysis, Hegel developed the concept of the Infinite in a way which further extended its critical function for religious discourse about God: from now on, the only understanding of God that can be called monotheistic in the strict sense will be that which is able to conceive the one God not merely as transcending the world; at the same time, this "God beyond" must be understood as immanent in the world.

I am able to follow Hegel yet one step further. He realized that the absoluteness that is contained within the true concept of the Infinite is not yet sufficiently captured through a definition of the Infinite alone. Recall Descartes's comment that we intend something "positive to the highest degree" with the expression *the Infinite*, even though the linguistic form of the expression is negative. Hegel's position is similiar. On the one hand, Hegel could describe religion in a global fashion as the ascent above the finite to the concept of the Infinite and, in general, could speak in one breath of the Infinite and the Absolute. On the other hand, in his *Logic* he treats the concept of the Infinite within the logic of Being, thereby implying that it is merely a relatively undifferentiated category of the Absolute. Such a move suggests that Hegel judged the category of the Infinite to have rather limited assertorical force, a conclusion that is consonant with the criticisms we raised above of Descartes's use of the intuition (or perhaps better, the feeling) of the Infinite as providing knowledge of God.

Moreover, reflection on this primordial datum of consciousness, on the limitation of all finite representations by an awareness of the Infinite that precedes them, does not yet overcome the distance between the Infinite and the notion of God employed within religion. It also does not allow us to conceive the Infinite as the source of everything that is different from it. It is of course possible (with Descartes) to derive the notion of a highest perfection from the idea of the Infinite and, from the notion of perfection, to obtain the further notion of necessary existence. Or perhaps necessary existence can be derived more simply from the idea of the Infinite by means of the concept of absoluteness which infinity implies. Still, none of these concepts yet entails the idea of an *existing being* [*Wesen*] that possesses infinity, absolute perfection, and necessary existence.

Now it is possible that this shortcoming could be overcome through the proofs of the existence of God—in particular through the cosmological proof, which moves back from the contingency of the finite to a "necessary" being, that is, one which exists through itself and can thus be conceived only as infinite. In my opinion, Kant is incorrect in claiming that the cosmological proof already presupposes the ontological proof; Hegel also challenged Kant's assertion. Nonetheless, thinkers have rightly challenged the claim that the cosmological proof leads to the idea of God, unless the idea of God has already been given from another source. For instance, the concept of a necessary being, taken in and of itself, could also be predicated of matter. Only if the idea of God has already been supplied is it possible to show that the representation of the one God necessarily implies the elements of infinity, absoluteness, highest perfection, and necessary existence. Moreover, without it one could not prove that these qualities can be attributed to no other being than the one God. Taken by itself, the cosmological argument does not supply what is needed; the bare category of the Infinite supplies even less.

Reflection on the concept of the Infinite does lead to the category of absoluteness. But in making this move, we have already gone far beyond what is explicitly contained within the category of the Infinite. Likewise, we move beyond the category of the Absolute when we attempt to clarify what is requisite for absoluteness. For the latter connotes not only self-sufficiency, in the sense of independence from all else, but also that everything else (if there is anything else) be thought as proceeding from the Absolute—and not only as proceeding from it according to a law foreign to the Absolute, but as produced through the Absolute itself, as the expression of itself. The true content of the idea of the Absolute is thus not yet expressed by the mere category of the Absolute as that which is self-sufficient and closed off from what is other. Instead, according to Hegel, this content is first fully expressed in the concept of *Spirit*, which essentially connotes a revealing, an expressing, of itself. Likewise, the content of the Infinite is first fully explicated in the concept of Spirit, insofar as that concept mediates the opposition between infinity and finitude, as we already saw to be demanded by the concept of the true Infinite.

Our reflection on the concept of the Absolute as the condition of absoluteness thus leads us to concede at least two points to Hegel's analysis in his *Logic*. First, a unity of the Absolute with its other, that is, with what is finite and limited, is required, such that this other is conceived as the expression of the Absolute. Second, this move goes beyond what is contained in the category of the Absolute, taken by itself. Of course, there is room to doubt whether the true content of the Absolute is appropriately expressed by Hegel's concept of the Concept and, in its final version, by his concepts of Idea and Spirit. In the case of the Concept, doubt is raised by the fact that, in contrast to other categories treated in his *Logic*, Hegel is forced oddly to overextend the

concept of the Concept—which should be described phe-
nomenologically and grounded in our everyday use of language—in order to be able to represent it as integrating the
moments which remain unreconciled in the final stages of
the "Logic of Essence."

Hegel's problems with Concept in the *Logic* are reminis-
cent of his problems in the *Phenomenology of Spirit* with the
concept of self-consciousness. Concept and self-consciousness (or ego) are, then, also linked very closely together for
Hegel. The dubiousness of his concept of Spirit, however, is
caused by the fact that it is developed from the phenomenon
of self-consciousness.[18] Hegel's concept of Spirit is grounded
in the structure of self-consciousness and is defined as the
knowledge of oneself attained through the other of oneself.
But it remains doubtful whether such a concept will be able
to integrate the content of the category of the Absolute and
the unity of the Absolute with its other. It was no mere
misunderstanding when Feuerbach viewed this concept of
Spirit as a hypostatization of the human self-consciousness.
In the light of our acknowledgment of the more positive
elements in Hegel's "Logic of Being" and "Logic of Essence,"
we should conclude more cautiously: the concept of Spirit
has perhaps remained somewhat metaphorical in Hegel, a
sort of augmentation of the Idealist idea of subjectivity that
is oriented around self-consciousness.

By introducing the concept of Spirit, Hegel was attempt-
ing to bring to conceptual expression the idea of God presupposed by the Christian religion and, more specifically, the
Christian doctrine of the Trinity. In so doing, he could appeal
to a theological tradition in Western Christendom that can be
traced back as far as Augustine. This school approached the

---

18. On this question see my "Der Geist und sein anderes," in
*Hegels Logik der Philosophie. Religion und Philosophie in der Theorie des
absoluten Geistes*, ed. Dieter Henrich and Rolf-Peter Horstmann (Stuttgart: Klett-Cotta, 1984), pp. 151-59.

dogma of the Trinity through the phenomenon of self-consciousness, which was understood as an image of the Trinitarian God. Later, after Anselm of Canterbury, the tradition reconstructed this dogma in the sense of the following phenomenon: in that the one God thinks himself, he gives rise to the Son, and he knows and loves the Other of himself in the Son *as* himself through the Spirit. As a result, in the tradition's speculative doctrine of the Trinity the Spirit had only the limited function of unifying what is different, whereas in Hegel's work Spirit plays a role throughout the entire process of self-consciousness—in postulating the opposed elements as well as in bringing about their unity.

Despite this difference, Hegel's interpretation of the doctrine of the Trinity according to the model of self-consciousness stands firmly within the theological tradition of Western Christendom. Consequently, it is understandable that he would have claimed to have brought the Christian idea of God to conceptual expression by means of his particular concept of the Absolute as Spirit. Nonetheless, Christian theology, even when it interpreted the doctrine of the Trinity psychologically, never completely lost its awareness that such interpretations produce only a picture of the Trinitarian relations, a picture that in many respects remains inadequate to its ultimate object.

The inadequacy of Hegel's view cannot be discussed here in detail. Clearly, the sources of the doctrine of the Trinity, in the relationship of Jesus to the Father and in the glorification of the Father and Son through the Spirit, cannot be reduced to the self-differentiating acts of a single divine subject. Instead, they have their point of departure in the divine confirmation of Jesus' eschatological message by means of his resurrection from the dead. According to the biblical sources of the doctrine of the Trinity, the *reciprocity* in the relation between the Father and Son (as also, analogously, in the relations among Father, Son, and Spirit) remains fundamental; it may not be reinterpreted in a "subordinarian" fashion as if the dependence moved only in one direction. Certainly, the Son acknowledges the Father as source and receives everything from him. Nevertheless, the Father is Father only in his relationship to the Son, and both are what they are only in the testimony of the Spirit, who, however, proceeds from the Father and is given *to* the Son as well as being imparted *through* him.

The understanding of "Spirit" in the case of the God of religion—at least for the biblical God—does not imply above all a divine intellect or a divine self-consciousness but rather God's creative power. The God of religion is experienced primarily as a will that manifests itself in history, as the will of a holy power and hence as personal. This phenomenon does *not* immediately imply the presupposition of a divine intellect and of a cooperation of will and intellect. In fact, such predicates may already be the products of an anthropomorphic interpretation. Awareness of this fact may have diminished within the theology of the early Church and the Middle Ages under the influence of Platonic and Aristotelian concepts of God as *nous;* yet it has remained alive precisely in its application to the doctrine of the Trinity. Like Lessing before him, Hegel was not in fact fully aware of the metaphorical elements in all such reflection.

Gaining insight into this fact can have a liberating influence on theologians. For it makes it possible to grant the correctness of those (beginning with Feuerbach) who criticize Hegel for the hypostatizations within his doctrine of Spirit, without thereby having to bring the entire tradition of philosophical theology to its collapse, as Feuerbach did. At the same time, the preceding analysis helps to overcome the impression in Hegel's *Logic* of a line of argumentation that is brazenly closed off from criticism. This may have been an impression that Hegel himself wanted to foster; still, abandoning such claims to immunity from criticism can only serve to increase interest in his philosophy.

The result of our inquiry for the philosophical concept

of the Absolute and its relationship to the God of religion is clear: philosophical reflection can lead to the formulation of criteria for presenting the understanding of God within a religious tradition. But it cannot actually replace the tradition. The metaphysics of the Absolute would do well to consider this fact in combination with a comparative discussion of the understanding of God in the various religious traditions. When metaphysics begins to explicate the understanding of God within a particular religious tradition—as occurred in Hegel's philosophy of religion and in the later philosophy of Schelling—it actually becomes theology. However, without actually taking this step, metaphysics can still discuss the significance of the general criteria drawn from metaphysical reflection on the Absolute for our understanding of finite being. After all, it is for the sake of this task—the task of achieving a comprehensive interpretation of the finite world—that metaphysics attempts to rise above the multiplicity of the finite toward the idea of the One, a One that grounds the unity of the world and provides the unifying context for the multitude of things within the world.

CHAPTER 3

SELF-CONSCIOUSNESS AND SUBJECTIVITY

ACCORDING TO a widely accepted modern view, individuals are persons not only as subjects of their actions but also as subjects of the contents of their self-consciousnesses. The "I," of which we are aware in self-consciousness because of its identity with our "self," has been accepted since Kant as the foundation for the unity of human experience. More precisely: the *unity* of this ego is taken to be the condition for synthesizing the manifold of intuitions into the unity of a particular consciousness of experience.[1]

Many have taken this phenomenon as sufficient for viewing the ego as the transcendental subject of all experience of objects in general, so that the experience of objects would be possible only for such a subject. Actually, if we look at it more closely, this may well not have been Kant's own position.[2] For

---

1. Immanuel Kant, *Critique of Pure Reason*, B 132-33.

2. See my *Anthropology in Theological Perspective*, trans. Matthew O'Connell (Philadelphia: Westminster, 1985), pp. 219-20. German edition: *Anthropologie in theologischer Perspektive* (Göttingen: Vandenhoeck & Ruprecht, 1983), pp. 212-13. See also Dieter Henrich, *Identität und Objektivität. Eine Untersuchung über Kants transzendentale Deduktion* (Heidelberg: C. Winter, 1976).

43

Kant, it is not the consciousness of objects in general but only the unity in our experience of objects that requires the unity of the "I" that thinks as its foundation. But what would our awareness of objects be without the ability to draw comparative distinctions, an ability which first makes it possible to conceive of an object in its distinctiveness? Hence, the view that the unity of self-consciousness is the condition for the consciousness of objects finds at any rate strong support in Kant's description of the functions of the understanding.

Interestingly, we do not find anything like this conception of the subjectivity of the human ego until the seventeenth or eighteenth century. In premodern metaphysical thought, the human soul was one entity alongside others; although it was the medium for experiencing all other entities, it was not the basis of their reality. Descartes has been taken as the founder of modern subjectivism. Yet even he viewed the ego of the *cogito,* along with all the other elements of our experience in the world, as dependent upon God, not only in reality but also in our consciousness.[3]

Admittedly, Locke and Berkeley did trace the awareness of objects back to the processing of sense data by our understanding, the "operations of the mind." Yet they did not take the individual consciousness as the basis for the construction of mundane experience—even though one reads in Locke: "When we hear, smell, taste, feel, meditate, or will anything, we know that we do so."[4] Kant was the first thinker who declared our awareness of the identity of the ego to be the basic condition of the possibility of our experience of objects.[5] He thus arrived at the epochal position, frequently

---

3. René Descartes, *Discourse on Method and Meditations,* trans. Lafleur, pp. 101-2 (= *Meditationes de prima philosophia,* 1st ed., pp. 28-29 [*Med.* III, §§ 23-24]).

4. John Locke, *An Essay Concerning Human Understanding,* ed. A. C. Frazer ([1690], 1894), 1:449 (Book II, chap. 27, no. 11).

5. Henrich has shown that Kant's view was not yet free from

attributed to Descartes, of resting all knowledge of experience upon the foundation of the ego's consciousness.

In his *Wissenschaftslehre* of 1794, Fichte then made the attempt systematically to derive all forms of knowledge from self-consciousness. Unfortunately, in the context of dealing with the problem of the constitution of self-consciousness, he entangled himself in the dilemmas associated with the notion of an ego that posits itself.[6] Still, his thesis, that self-consciousness has constitutive significance for the possibility of our experience of objects, remained untouched by these difficulties. The thesis then found its classical expression in Hegel's formulation of the relationship between the consciousness of objects and the consciousness of self: "The truth of consciousness is the *self-consciousness*, and the latter is the ground of the former, such that in existence all consciousness of another object is self-consciousness. I know of an object that is mine (it is my representation); in so doing I know of myself."[7]

If self-consciousness were in fact the "ground" and the "truth" of all consciousness of objects, then the metaphysical question of the Absolute could indeed be raised only on the basis of human subjectivity. In this case, it would arise as a

---

internal tensions (see n. 2 above). Among the influences on Kant's position belongs Leibniz's doctrine of monads, along with Leibniz's belief that "all our phenomena, that is to say, all things which are ever able to happen to us, are only consequences of our being." See G. W. Leibniz, *Discourse on Method*, trans. George Montgomery (La Salle: Open Court, 1902), p. 24. French/German edition: *Discours de Métaphysique / Metaphysische Abhandlung*, trans. and ed. Herbert Herring, Philosophische Bibliothek, vol. 260 (Hamburg: Felix Meiner, 1958), no. 14 (p. 34).

6. See Dieter Henrich, *Fichtes ursprüngliche Einsicht* (Frankfurt: Klostermann, 1967).

7. G. W. F. Hegel, *Hegel's Philosophy of Nature: being Part Two of the Encyclopedia of the Philosophical Sciences*, trans. A. V. Miller (Oxford: Clarendon, 1970). German edition: *Encyclopädie* (1817), § 424. The last sentence comes from the comment *(Zusatz)* added to the 3rd German edition of 1830.

question posed by human subjectivity concerning the source that constitutes it. But then the subjectivity that inquires into its presupposed source would have to be conceived as simultaneously positing the idea of its own source. If we accept this framework, the claim that the Absolute precedes the subject will have to be abandoned and replaced by a focus on the activity of the subject itself, which then presupposes its own absolute ground.

In other words, on this analysis the step from Hegel to Feuerbach would appear to be the inevitable result of thinking the Idealist position through to its end in a consistent manner. Of course, Feuerbach did not overcome a remnant of Idealism, namely, the necessity that the finite subject presuppose for itself an absolute ground of itself. The motivation that Feuerbach suggests for presupposing God is surely the weakest element in his entire position, and the thinkers who followed him—from Marx and Nietzsche up to Durkheim and Freud—sought better grounds for the presupposition. Nonetheless, Feuerbach was right: if we begin with the thesis that self-consciousness is the "ground" and "truth" of all consciousness of objects, then every thought of an absolute ground of subjectivity must be the product of subjectivity. Consequently, the necessity of presupposing an Absolute could not be explicated (with regard to the content of this notion), without immediately running into the suspicion that we are dealing with a merely human projection.

What of the project of specifying the content of the idea of the Absolute? It appears possible only if the Spirit of which Hegel spoke is more than self-consciousness. For only then can we unmask the claim that its absoluteness is a mere hypostatizing of the human self-consciousness conceived as limitless. To avoid this outcome, we must presuppose that the content of our awareness of objects is not reducible to the self-consciousness that represents itself in them. Even then, the idea of the Absolute remains an idea of humans, of beings who are conscious of themselves. Only if we resist the tendency to reduce the consciousness of objects to the activity of a self-consciousness, taking it instead as the foundation for the development of self-consciousness, will it be possible to provide content to the idea of the Absolute as the ground of everything finite, without as a result becoming hopelessly entangled in contradictions.

How can this be done? Over against the assumption of transcendental philosophy—that there is an ego which, as the condition of the unity of experience, precedes all experience and is conscious of itself—stands the thesis that the genesis of the ego lies within the process of experience itself. The latter position already has its roots in the eighteenth century, in the work of David Hume; indeed, a preliminary version can be found even earlier, in John Locke's view that the identity of persons depends on their awareness of themselves, and thus on memory.[8] Against Locke's view, Leibniz objected that one's own memory could not be the sole means for the constitution of personal identity, because one can be instructed by others concerning one's past life. In addition, he argued, one must distinguish between personal or moral identity and the physical identity of the ego.[9] But Locke had already noted the problems with the claim, implied by Leibniz's view, that there is an underlying "soul-substance," and Hume completely dispensed with the view, construing the consciousness of the self instead as momentary and as given only through perception.

For Hume, the self is primarily a "bundle" of impressions which accompany perception. The belief in the self's

---

8. John Locke, *Essay*, pp. 460ff. (Book II, chap. 27, nos. 19ff.).

9. G. W. Leibniz, *New Essays on Human Understanding*, trans. and ed. Peter Remnant and Jonathan Bennett (New York: Cambridge University Press, 1981), pp. 236-37. French/German edition: *Nouveaux essais sur l'entendement humain/Neue Abhandlungen über den menschlichen Verstand*, trans. and ed. W. von Engelhardt and H. H. Holz (Frankfurt: Insel, 1961), Book II, chap. 27, §§ 9-10.

identity rests, as do all identity claims, on "some fiction or imaginary principle of union"—in this case, primarily on the productive function of memory, which constructs relations of similarity between impressions.[10] Hume did, however, admit that our awareness of the self's identity can be expanded beyond the scope of memory by means of the principle of causality. More importantly, he also acknowledged the inability of his account to explain the emergence of our consciousness of the identity of the self.[11] It is thus understandable that the transcendental, a priori account of the unity of the ego as the subject of experience could be viewed, even in Anglo-Saxon philosophy, as a solution for the unsolved problems in Hume's description. In fact, according to the testimony of John Dewey, William James was the first thinker to show that the assumption of a self "outside and behind" the stream of consciousness was completely superfluous.[12]

James dismissed the ego of Kant's transcendental apperception—when it is construed as the subject of experience—as a descent back into the old metaphysics of the soul: "if it be so, transcendentalism is only substantialism grown shame-faced, and the Ego only a 'cheap and nasty' edition of the soul."[13] He himself modified Hume's concep-

---

10. David Hume, *A Treatise of Human Nature,* ed. L. A. Selby-Bigge and P. H. Niddich (Oxford: Clarendon, [1739], 1978), pp. 252, 261, 262 (Bk. I, Pt. 4, sect. 6): "the memory not only discovers the identity, but also contributes to its production, by producing the relation of resemblance among the perceptions."

11. In the Appendix to vol. 2 of *Treatise of Human Nature* (1740), pp. 635-36.

12. John Dewey, "The Ego as Cause" (1894), in *Philosophy, Psychology and Social Practice,* ed. Joseph Ratner (New York: Putnam, 1963), p. 207 n. 4. Here Dewey, who until around 1890 himself stood under the influence of Kant and Hegel, says that James "indeed has given that theory [the assumption of a transcendental subject] the hardest knocks it has yet received from the psychological side."

13. William James, *The Principles of Psychology,* ed. G. H. Miller (Cambridge: Harvard University Press, [1890], 1983), p. 345.

tion by means of the notion that every new, momentary feeling of the ego integrates and appropriates all the moments of the ego that preceded it. Whereas the self whom we know ourselves to be encompasses everything that we connect with our physical existence, including its social and spiritual relations, the ego, which is aware of this self as its own, is "a *Thought*, at each moment different from that of the last moment, but *appropriative* of the latter with all that the latter called its own."[14] With this move, James bound together the synthetic point of view, drawn from the Idealist doctrine of the transcendental subject, with the momentary nature of the self stressed by Hume, who held that the awareness of the self is given along with the series of moments of experience. James was thus able, on the one hand, to do greater justice to the consciousness of the ego's identity than Hume had done, and, on the other, to conceptualize this identity as growing and changing through the succession of the moments and phases of the self's experience.

With his distinction between Ego and Self, and with his view of self-consciousness as a self-identification that integrates a sequence of acts, James was able to create a model that offers a viable interpretative framework for contemporary research into the process of identity construction. Indeed, we can evaluate the social psychology of George Herbert Mead, which stresses the significance of social relationships for the formation and development of the individual sense of identity,[15] only against the background of James's distinction between the Ego and Self and his notion of the "social self."

Mead's elaboration of James's theory converged with the initial efforts of the Freudian school toward a theory of

---

14. Ibid., p. 379.

15. George Herbert Mead, *Mind, Self and Society* (Chicago: University of Chicago Press, 1934). Compare my discussion of Mead's position in *Anthropology*, pp. 185-90.

identity construction; this convergence then inspired Erik Erikson to link the psychoanalytic theory of the ego with Mead's social psychology in his description of the process of identity formation.[16] Unfortunately, both Mead and Erikson had, in comparison to James, a rather hazy conception of the ego as the subject of any given process of identification. Some rather peculiar inconsistencies result. For instance, although Mead and Erikson acknowledge a plurality of changing conceptions of the individual self, they do not provide a theoretical treatment of change within the ego that is said to bring about the identification—even though an identity of ego and self is supposed to result from the completion of this process of identification.

On this last point, James's position finds a clearer reflection in the linguistic-analytic interpretation and employment of the word "I" as an index word or "indexical," a word that refers to whoever is speaking at the time.[17] Linguistic analysis here confirms the insight of Hume and his modern followers: the empirical starting point for our talk of the ego has the character of a momentary instance that is posited along with the subject matter of our discourse or perceptions at any given time.[18] Unfortunately, these thinkers often neglect the other fact—which James, working within the Lockean tradition, emphasized—that the consciousness of the "I" refers back to earlier situations when this word was used by "the same" person. The consciousness of the "I" depends on the past in two senses: that of the bodily identity of the self, along with all the connotations of the "social" and "spiritual" being of the self that depend on the body; and that of the active

---

16. See my *Anthropology*, pp. 191-200.

17. So also Gilbert Ryle, *The Concept of Mind* (London: Hutchinson, 1949), p. 188. Cf. my *Anthropology*, pp. 206ff.

18. For relevant essays by G. E. Moore, C. D. Broad, and Bertrand Russell, see the anthology *Self-Knowledge and Self-Identity*, ed. Sidney Shoemaker (Ithaca: Cornell University Press, 1963), pp. 48ff.

principle that expresses itself in the act of speaking and calls itself "I."

In both senses memory plays an essential role in the process of appropriating the earlier moments of the ego from the standpoint of the present moment.[19] Our consciousness of identity, which is implicated in every use of the word "I," is closely tied to this phenomenon. But simply appealing to memory does not yet explain how the relationship between present and past is actually established; it is rather presupposed as the content of memory. Indeed, even the interpretation of memory as productive, as the appropriation in each individual instant—though it may be able to explain how an already established identity is modified within the further course of experience—is not able to explain its original constitution. The succession of instants of ego-awareness does not yet result in the related awareness of the *unity* of the ego, the identity that preserves itself through the further course of time.[20]

In contrast to James, Bergson described the life of consciousness as a *duration* that overlaps various temporal moments. According to his view, not only the ego's consciousness of identity but every act of perception is characterized by the fact that "the individual moments are extended into and fused with one another."[21] Bergson attributed this

---

19. William James, *Psychology*, pp. 378-79. Cf. Henri Ey, *Consciousness*, trans. John H. Flodstrom (Bloomington: Indiana University Press, 1978), pp. 278-79. French edition: *La conscience* (Paris: Presses universitaires de France, 1963). German edition: *Das Bewußtsein* (Berlin, 1967), pp. 244-45. According to Ey, the ego or self "constitutes itself through its own historical memory" (p. 197; cf. p. 118).

20. Henri Ey takes a similar position concerning the problem of the unity of the consciousness; see ibid., pp. 36-38.

21. Henri Bergson, *Matter and Memory*, trans. Nancy Margaret Paul and W. Scott Palmer (New York: Zone Books, 1988). French edition: *Matière et mémoire: Essai sur la relation du corps à l'esprit* (Geneva: Éditions Albert Skira, [1909], 1946). German edition: *Materie und Gedächtnis* (Berlin, 1964), p. 65; cf. p. 98.

achievement of the ego, which is fundamental for the human perception of forms [Gestalten], to the function of memory; and certainly it would not be possible without memory. Nevertheless, while memory and recollection are directed toward the past, aiming to retrieve once-received information and to make it present, the perception of the time-overlapping identity of a form also involves the awareness of a pure present. That is, in contrast to Bergson's concept of "pure duration,"[22] perceiving identity involves a consciousness of duration that is not aware of the flow of time. In fact, Bergson's favorite example of pure duration, the hearing of a melody, is, as the perception of a gestalt, more closely related to duration in the sense of a time-overlapping act of bringing various temporal moments into the present than it is to a stream into which we abandon ourselves.

Bergson's concept of duration thus melds together two very different elements, which must be conceptually distinguished. In fact, the experience of the stream itself seems to rely upon the awareness of impressions of gestalts that are present as time-overlapping, as well as owing its continuity to this awareness. For the impressions of gestalts always arise within the horizon of a perceptual field, which Maurice Merleau-Ponty has termed the "field of presence."[23]

---

22. Henri Bergson, *Time and Free Will: An Essay on the Immediate Data of Consciousness*, trans. F. L. Pogson (New York: Macmillan, 1959), pp. 86-87, 99ff. French edition: *Essai sur les données immédiates de la conscience* (1889), in *Oeuvres* (Paris: Presses universitaires de France, 1970), pp. 59 and 67 (in 1889 edition, pp. 64 and 74).

23. Maurice Merleau-Ponty, *Phenomenology of Perception*, trans. Colin Smith (London: Routledge, 1970), p. 415. French edition: *Phénoménologie de la perception* (Paris: Gallimard, 1945), pp. 475ff. For a discussion of the concept of field, see, e.g., pp. 15-17 (pp. 23- 25 in French); see also Aron Gurwitsch, *The Field of Consciousness* (Pittsburgh: Duquesne University Press, 1964). French edition: *Théorie du champ de la conscience* (Paris: Desclée de Brouwer, 1957). See also Henri Ey, *Consciousness*, pp. 86-199.

The far-reaching implications of this conclusion will be discussed below, when we come to the question of the experience of time and its relationship to eternity. First, consider again the question of how the ego's identity is established through its awareness of objects. It is sufficient at this point to appeal to the unity of the forms or gestalts that we perceive and to the way that they are located within a perceptual field or "field of presence." It is clear that the consciousness of objects, when conceived in this manner, is not originally grounded in the consciousness of the ego and its identity. Instead, conversely, the formation of the individual ego is based, as Henri Ey has stressed, in the life of the consciousness and is to be understood as "its structural and historical result."[24] In the history of the individual, the development and training of the perceptual field (especially the awareness of the constancy of space) and the development of linguistic ability precede the emergence of the consciousness of the "I."[25]

These facts justify the conclusion that the consciousness of objects is, in principle, independent from self-consciousness. The identity of objects and, in the act of perception, their relatedness within the unity of the field of presence, do not rest upon the unity of some "existing and enduring" ego [Kant]. Rather, consciousness of the ego's unity is mediated through experience of the world, insofar as this experience allows the ego to become aware of its own body as existing within the context of a world and to construct a social and spiritual self in connection with it. This is the self to which one refers when one says "I." We may assume that the consciousness of the selfsameness of the ego in the medium of memory is always mediated through an awareness of the identity of the self. The self, for its part, is anchored within the framework of worldly experience and experiences its

---

24. Ey, *Consciousness*, p. 23.
25. See also Gordon W. Allport, *Pattern and Growth in Personality* (New York: Holt, Rinehart and Winston, 1961), p. 112.

full development, its crises and changes, within the horizon of such experience.

Once the individual ego has been formed—say, roughly at fifteen months, when the child is not only able to recognize its own body parts and body as its own, but has also learned to use the word "I"—then it can move beyond its own field of presence, becoming the point of reference for remembered events and the experiences of earlier life phases. Of course, the individual ego is in no way the only such reference point. The more stable the order of one's life-world with its familiar objects, the more important a role will be played by the perception of objects which are not encountered as merely subjective. The more strongly determined by tradition the linguistically mediated awareness of cultural order, and the greater the agreement between individuals within a social community regarding the foundations of the natural world and of the social order, the more firm will be the basis for the unfolding of individual particularity and individual aware-ness of identity. People's room to maneuver need not be narrowed because of sharing a social context; it is a question of the complexity of the cultural world.

At any rate, the framework provided by the cultural world does not rest upon the identity of an existing and enduring ego within the consciousness of individuals. We do not need to posit such an ego as the condition for tying together the multiplicity of our experience; this function is performed by the unity of the life-world, which is given in the cultural consciousness and conveyed through the me-dium of collective recollection. Collective recollection is pri-marily concerned not with the ego, but rather with the objects of experience and with their context in the world. A con-sciousness of the subjectivity of one's experience arises only to the extent that one experiences a deviation from the com-mon framework.

This sort of stable world has often had its basis within religion. Only when the basis was destroyed, as in Europe in the seventeenth century, did it become necessary to derive a new way of establishing this world. Thus, Western thinkers began to seek a foundation for the social order in the concept of the unity of human nature, and a foundation for the multiplicity of experiences of the world in the unity of self-consciousness.

Self-consciousness could take on this function because the ego of grown humans, which maintains identity with itself through memory, has always provided a reference point for bringing unity to particular individual experiences within the context of an individual's life history. A more specific example is provided by the association of individual knowledge claims with the sense or consciousness of knowing. Through this association, the consciousness of knowing stands in a much closer relationship to self-consciousness than does simple perceptual awareness, which depends completely upon the perceived form of its object.

Note that the close link between knowledge and self-consciousness has not always been foundational for the concept of knowledge. In early Greek thought, knowledge was understood to be a seeing of that which rests in itself alone. Even in Plato's thought, the moment of insight, despite all the necessary human preparations for it, still has the character of seeing; its certainty depends completely upon the immutability of the intuited ideas. In this theory of knowledge, the identity of the ideas does not rest upon the identity of the intuiting consciousness, but, conversely, the imperishability of the ideas serves as the basis, so that the soul that knows them can participate in their imperishability.[26] Even the immortality of the gods "is nourished" from the intuition or "science" of the ideas.[27] By the time of Aristotle and the Stoics,

---

26. Plato *Phaedo* 79e 2-3, in *Plato: The Collected Dialogues*, ed. Edith Hamilton and Huntington Cairns (Princeton: Princeton University Press, 1961).

27. Plato *Phaedrus* 247d 1ff.

knowledge and science had become much more unambiguously matters of the human soul and of its striving for knowledge. Still, only when the Christian Aristotelianism of the Middle Ages transformed Aristotle's active reason from a superhuman quantity to a human potentiality of the soul were the presuppositions fully in place for making the human soul the only basis and guarantor of knowledge. This process of transformation was thus an important step on the way to the emergence of the modern conception of subjectivity.

Seen no longer as the product of the cosmic Logos at work in the soul, science—understood not as intuitive but as proceeding argumentatively and discursively—is in fact dependent upon the unity of consciousness as the ground for the unity of argumentation. Because the awareness of knowing, in contrast to simple perceptual awareness, always includes an awareness of the subject of such knowing, the unitary consciousness that underlies the unity of argumentation is characterized by a unity of *self*-consciousness. This unity need not be present in the sense of the identity of the individual empirical ego, but it must be posited at least as an identity of the subject that is engaged in doing science. Empirical subjects take part in the scientific view of the world to the extent that they fulfill these conditions. Hence, the unity of self-consciousness always underlies the activity of arguing about various subjects and drawing connections between them.

So the Kantian thesis—that a transcendental apperception and a transcendental subject are conditions for the unity, if not of experience itself, then at least of the modern type of empirical-scientific knowledge of the world and the self— was not simply manufactured out of thin air. Still, it is necessary to determine the boundaries to the scope of this thesis. Some of these boundaries stem from the foregoing discussion; they can be presented in three points:

First, the [Kantian] thesis that the identity of self-consciousness is the condition for the unity of experience does not apply to the experience of the world which precedes the forming and solidifying of the ego within the individual. Instead, the experience of the world, along with the child's developing awareness of the constancy of space and of language, is itself the condition for the formation of the individual ego. The ego first arises as a momentary quantity and only attains stability through a long process of identity construction, mediated by the continually existing self of one's own body and by the related units of significance, the social self and the ego ideal. For this reason alone, the identity produced by the consciousness of the ego cannot be the condition of experience in general.

Second, even in the case of adults one cannot reckon without reservation upon a stable and unchanging identity of self-consciousness without deviations, exceptions, or suppressions. The idea that an existing and enduring ego is the condition for the unity of conscious experience must for this reason be judged to be an idealized construction—however well it serves to provide a unitary basis for the modern scientific description of the world as encountered within the secular empirical sciences.

Third, the unity of self-consciousness is not the sole conceivable and demonstrable basis for the unity of conscious experience; therefore, it is also not the necessary condition for the unity of experience in general. Viewed historically, the comprehensive unity of experience was first formulated in the communal consciousness that the cosmic and social order had been grounded through the activity of divine powers. Is it not possible that an awareness of a comprehensive unity of the experienced world could also have been achieved in this way?

The findings of human cultural history give overwhelming support to this assumption. Of course, it could be that at the basis of these cultural-historical antecedents one will find a hidden psychological mechanism, which only Kant's transcendental reflection will be able to bring to light.

Yet even the first two points listed above are sufficient to destroy the basis that would be required for such a construal of cultural history. These points required us to place restrictions on the assumption that a transcendental subject is the condition for the unity of experience in view of the individual historical process of acquiring experience. To make the contrary point, one would have to assume, as valid without exception, that an existing and enduring ego is the condition for the unity of experience, and would have to appeal to the constitution of experiential awareness as we actually observe it. For only such an assumption could compel us to affirm, against the self-testimony of ancient cultures, that this mechanism also explains the genesis of their conscious states.

It is certainly true that the idealized assumption of a unity of consciousness functions as the basis for the unity of the empirical-scientific description of the world. Suppose that our goal is to present cultural history in the spirit and within the context of such an empirical-scientific description of the world. Would it then follow, when we are reconstructing the world-consciousness of ancient culture, that we are justified in assuming that the unity of self-consciousness was also for them the basis for the unity of experience? Could this unified self-consciousness have been the actual source from which they derived their representations of how the gods function to establish the unity of the world? But this criticism must also be rejected. The theory of a transcendental subjectivity cannot explain the process of formation by which an individual ego first arises and attains stability. One is not justified in making the counterfactual assumption that from the very beginning an existing and enduring ego already existed, an ego that makes possible both the emergence of the consciousness of a unified world and the acquisition of language.

Moreover, the assumption that transcendental subjectivity is the condition for the unity of the empirical-scientific understanding of the world is itself historically conditioned.

This is the case not only insofar as it presupposes the separation of the modern empirical sciences from their theological antecedents in the inherited picture of the world and humankind, but also in view of the further development of the modern empirical sciences themselves. Already in the last century, the Neo-Kantians debated whether the post-Kantian stabilization of methodological awareness in the sciences is able to provide a sufficient unity for the empirical reality that they described. Hence, Kant's teaching that transcendental (self-)consciousness is the condition for the unity of experience is, perhaps, merely the expression of a particular historical epoch within the development of scientific reason and philosophical reflection on the sciences. Of course, as with all great philosophical thought, this does not exclude the possibility that his teaching may still have something to say to later ages. However, it cannot be adopted in its original form, but only within a broader hermeneutical framework, one conditioned by the experiences and questions of a later historical period.

The contemporary philosophical treatment of human subjectivity will therefore have to extend its borders beyond the critique of reason presented by Kant and the theories of subjectivity advanced within German Idealism. This treatment will have to consider the developmental-psychological conditions for the emergence of the ego within the life of the individual and for its linguistic mediation. It must pay attention to the social conditions for identity construction, understood as a long process of the stabilization of subjectivity. Finally, it may no longer neglect the cultural-historical and religious conditions for the emergence of subjectivity as a human form of life.

Some of the initial moves in the direction of broadening out the interpretative framework for the phenomenon of subjectivity were already made within German Idealism. Hegel did consider this mediation (of the identity of self-consciousness through the other of itself) in its relation to the world, and particularly within the social context. Yet he described these relations as *self*-mediations, in the sense that, for him, the starting point of the process always lies within self-consciousness and its activity, leaving the mediation to take on the form of an externalization and return to oneself. The constitution of self-consciousness based on the relationship with the other of oneself thus remains unexplained— especially since, for Hegel, even Spirit always has the form of self-consciousness.

Johann Gottlieb Fichte suggested a way out of this circle, after having become aware of the inadequacy of the idea that the ego posits itself through its own activities and the impossibility of basing experiential knowledge in this idea. But Fichte could not allow that subjectivity might be constituted within the realm of worldly experience since, for him as for others in the tradition of Kant, such experience already depended on the unity of the ego's consciousness. The constitution of subjectivity, understood as the unity of self-consciousness, could therefore be based only upon a source beyond the world.

But what happens when all empirical knowledge is viewed as conditioned by the unity of an ego—which then, of course, must already have been constituted? It was clear that the source of the ego could not be characterized using the language of empirical experience but only using the language of religious mysticism. Historical Christianity came to be employed only as an illustration of this state of affairs, and the religious constitution of subjectivity was no longer acknowledged as historically mediated. But we have found reason to question the claim that the unity of all experience— and thus also the content of "experience in general"—is already conditioned by the unity of an ego that remains identical with itself. By challenging this assumption, we remove the barriers that had blocked inquiry into how the ego might be constituted through experience in the world—and thus through the religious traditions that arise in the context of such experience.

In any contemporary philosophical account of the constitution of subjectivity, some consideration of the genesis of the subject is absolutely indispensable. In such an inquiry, everything points toward one question: Is the constitution of individual subjectivity adequately explained by reference to its interactions within the social context, or does it require us to ascend above the context of society? The latter approach would allow us to explain the roots of a society's cultural identity, the constitution of individual subjectivity, *and* the individual's ability occasionally to turn against society out of motives that need not be solely egotistical.

At this point, we begin to discern the connections between the metaphysical problem of ascending to the concept of the Absolute, and the issues involved with the constitution of subjectivity and the foundations of cultural unity within a society. Clearly, the question of the Absolute is framed too narrowly if it is approached solely on the basis of the subjectivity theme, especially if the development of the individual ego is already mediated through a process of worldly experience. Nevertheless, it is precisely the subjective conditions for experience in the world—conditions that are pivotal not only for the history of science but also for the scientific description of the world—which provide the point of departure for an ascent beyond that which is merely given within the world. By concentrating on these conditions, we can gain insight into the origins of the human world *and* the ego (hence also of the cultural order) in the Absolute. When we thematize such phenomena, we discover renewed relevance in the concepts of premodern metaphysics, including the metaphysics of antiquity, in which the topics of world, humankind, and society were still bound together at their very roots. These approaches still have much to offer, even if their contemporary appropriation must be adapted to the altered discursive situation of modern consciousness.

The metaphysics of the Absolute that I am proposing would not merely attempt, on the grounds of subjectivity, to reconstrue the constitution of the subject through some source in the Absolute that precedes it. Instead, it would carry out the "rising above" toward the idea of the Absolute from a starting point that encompasses worldly experience, self-consciousness, and their reciprocal mediation. Only this type of metaphysics is able to avoid the suspicion that the idea of the Absolute involves only an emasculated mirror image of self-consciousness. As long as self-consciousness is conceived as the ground and truth of all the contents of consciousness, it falls unavoidably to such suspicion. If, however, the development and stabilization of the ego's identity are themselves already mediated through the process of worldly experience, the themes of philosophical theology can no longer be quite so casually dismissed.

What place, then, should be granted to the subjectivity theme within the framework of this effort to find a new foundation for the metaphysics of the Absolute? Every conception of the absolute One must today prove its worth by showing itself to be not only the source and completion of the world but also the constitutive ground and highest good of subjectivity. Only in this fashion can a contemporary metaphysics of the Absolute do justice to the state of the problem as it has been presented in modern thought. For the highest form of independent existence within the realm of the finite is the subjectivity of the being who is characterized by awareness and self-consciousness. Consequently, it is crucial that a newly rethought metaphysics must conceive the Absolute as the source and goal of finite subjectivity. The Absolute must be understood not as standing in contradiction to the independence of the finite, which finds its fullest expression in subjectivity, but instead precisely as the completion and perfection [*Vollendung*] of the relationship of the Infinite and Absolute to the existence of the finite and to the finite world in general.

This is no simple task. Consider the concepts of preservation and self-preservation. These concepts, developed during the emergence of modern thought, certainly belong to the prehistory of the subjectivity theme. The difficulties they raise are revealed in some of the more recent attempts to interpret this theme and the role it played in the seventeenth century. For example, Hans Blumenberg has explored the concept of a natural striving toward self-preservation that is endemic to every being, a concept first presented in the work of Campanella and further developed in the seventeenth century especially by Hobbes and Spinoza. Blumenberg links this concept to the tendency, expressed in the law of inertia, for matter to continue to exist, interpreting it as antithetical to the Christian doctrine that all finite beings depend upon their Creator for their continued existence. The striving for self-preservation allegedly makes superfluous the external activity of God aimed at preserving the creation; it replaces such external activity with self-affirmation.[28]

In opposition to Blumenberg, Dieter Henrich has correctly shown that the concept of self-preservation already implies a dependence upon preservation in general, and therefore an understanding of existence as finite and dependent. A being that exists out of and through itself needs no preservation, not even self-preservation. The striving for self-preservation is, in the first place, only the indication of a being that is related to itself in the light of the need that its existence has for preservation. But it cannot mean that the being that works for and is concerned with its own preservation is no longer dependent upon some sort of outside preservation. Quite the opposite: Every need for preservation already implies that one lacks full self-control over the conditions of one's own existence. Hence the striving for self-preservation already presupposes that a being is preserved

---

28. Hans Blumenberg, "Selbsterhaltung und Beharrung. Zur Konstitution der neuzeitlichen Rationalität," in *Subjektivität und Selbsterhaltung. Beiträge zur Diagnose der Moderne*, ed. Hans Ebeling (Frankfurt: Suhrkamp, 1976), pp. 144-207, esp. pp. 156-57.

through whatever entity on which its existence is dependent. One must certainly grant that any being which is able to establish a relationship to itself and to the conditions of its own existence, and which strives to maintain itself in existence, is actively involved in its own preservation; preservation is not simply imposed upon it from outside. But only this sort of preserving activity of a Creator would be ruled out by the acknowledgment of self-preservation. Conversely, the imposition theory would clearly be incompatible with any participation of the creation in its own preservation.

Instead, one has to conceive of the creative and preserving activity of God in such a manner that it has the independence of the creation in view. It must be an independence that plays a role in one's theoretical as well as one's practical self-relation to the conditions of one's own existence and its maintenance. Such independence through self-relationship, by the way, is not simply identical with the persistence of matter in whatever state a body is in at a given time—even if, with Newton and in contrast to Descartes, one understands such persistence as the expression of a power inherent in bodies themselves, a *vis insita*. In contrast to merely continuing to exist, self-preservation—in the full sense of an active self-relation—is possible only for a being that has a consciousness of itself, a point also defended by Henrich. We can speak of self-preservation on the part of prehuman life-forms only figuratively. Nonetheless, both the tendency of matter to persist in existence and the behaviors of prehuman life-forms that contribute to their preservation can be understood as steps in the direction of the stage reached by humankind: the independence of finite existence through self-preservation.[29]

---

29. Dieter Henrich, "Die Grundstruktur der modernen Philosophie," in ibid., pp. 97-121, esp. p. 111: "Whatever must preserve itself must know that it does not always and absolutely have its ground in itself." Henrich especially criticizes Heidegger's interpretation of the modern principle of the subjectivity of the self-consciousness as "self-

One is right to demand that any renewed metaphysics of the Absolute which claims to be relevant to modern consciousness must not be allowed to obscure the notion of human subjectivity, but must conceive the Absolute as the source and goal of this subjectivity. Yet this demand already implies a very particular view of the relationship between metaphysics and the philosophy of religion. A conception of the Absolute that places positive value on the independence of the finite to the extent of affirming the idea of self-preservation is no longer in harmony with the understandings of God found in all the world religions. Such a conception is opposed to all viewpoints that judge the independent existence of the finite to be mere appearance. Yet even those views that hold finite existence to be ephemeral stand deeply opposed to the phenomenon of self-preservation, because the intention underlying this notion must appear to them as, in the final analysis, of no avail. Not many religions attribute to individual existence—at least individual human existence—an eternal significance before God. Among them, certainly, is Christianity, with its eschatological hope for a resurrection of the dead. Resurrection rescues from mortality unique, individually existing humans who are linked with God, and awards them fellowship with the eternal God without subsuming their creaturely identity into the divine being.

This eternal affirmation of the individual existence of created beings, found in eschatology, makes its appearance as the final aim of the divine creative will. Even the distinctively Christian idea that God seeks a relationship with every one of his creatures with eternal love—an idea especially

---

powerful activity" (pp. 110-11). Cf. also p. 113; and, in the same volume, Henrich, "Über Selbstbewußtsein und Selbsterhaltung," pp. 122-43, esp. pp. 132ff. Henrich also criticizes Blumenberg for connecting the theme of self-preservation with the physical principle of inertia on the grounds that self-preservation presupposes a self-understanding (pp. 129ff.).

visible in the parables of the one sheep, the one son, and the one coin that were lost—is tied closely with the affirmation that finite creatures will continue to exist beyond death and throughout eternity, an affirmation that is central to Christian eschatology.

Hence it is certainly no coincidence that the idea of human subjectivity has been most fully developed within the circle of influence of the Christian religion. In part Christian theology laid the ground for this idea: through the emphasis on human freedom and human responsibility in patristic theology; through Augustine's psychology of the will; through the interpretation of Aristotle's active reason as a potential of the human soul in the Christian Aristotelianism of the Middle Ages. Campanella may have taken over the idea of self-preservation from the Stoic tradition; but even he reinterpreted it along Christian lines by linking it with the love of God, who is the preserver and perfecter of creation. The fact that this idea could serve in the seventeenth century to divorce anthropology from the theological tradition should not be ascribed to the motif of self-preservation as such (in contrast to outside preservation). Much more, its explanation lies in the task, faced by the thinkers of the seventeenth century, of providing an anthropological foundation for political philosophy in a manner that would be independent of the confessional antagonisms which were destroying the peace of society.

Not subjectivity per se but rather the attempt to make it independent of any relation to God stands in opposition to the Christian belief in creation. That such an attempt cannot be successful is revealed, in an exemplary fashion, by the failure of Fichte's endeavor, which sought to ground the constitution of the unity of self-consciousness in an action of the ego. Yet this project so perfectly fits the spirit of an age striving to emancipate itself from the Christian tradition that—despite Fichte's insight into the inevitability of its failure—it has survived into the present. It is at work, for instance, wherever the concept of action is employed as the fundamental concept of anthropology.[30]

Neither the problems of cultural anthropology, nor those of language, nor even the concept of history, can really be clarified in any fundamental fashion by means of the concept of action. To inflate the concept of action in this manner serves only to obscure its significant, though limited, anthropological function. Its limits are given by the fact that action always presupposes an acting subject. Action is thus tied to a structure that involves realizing ends by choosing and employing appropriate means. Only the time-bridging identity of the subject can ground and guarantee the unity of action beyond the context of individual processes that seek to realize specific ends. Neither the use of language nor an appeal to the entire process of experience within the world can ground the unity of action in this way. Instead, we can locate contexts of action within the use of language and within experience in the world that nonetheless remain subordinate to the more encompassing framework of language and to the always-new adventure of experience. As long as we move within individual frameworks of action, we exercise some control over our life, over our time, and over our environment. But the framework of control is never all-encompassing; it always remains embedded within a life-context that is formed by other factors.

Acting and subjectivity belong especially closely together. Nevertheless, human subjectivity is not fully exhausted in its guise as acting subject. The self-relation that characterizes subjectivity has not only a practical but also a theoretical aspect; and the theoretical takes precedence over

---

30. This position is held by A. Gehlen (discussed critically in my *Anthropology*, pp. 39ff.), but also within speech act theory (see ibid., pp. 361ff.) and the general theory of society since Max Weber, as well as in the theory of history (see ibid., pp. 504ff.; cf. pp. 408f. n. 18, and p. 473 n. 222).

the practical aspect, under whose compass action belongs. For the consciousness of one's own identity forms the framework for one's choice of goals or ends, and action is directed toward their realization. The choice of ends does not itself have the actual character of an action, unless the chosen ends are embedded from the outset within a broader framework of ends. The process of choosing an end is characterized by a coordination with one's own identity, just as the agent inevitably identifies herself with whatever ends she has chosen.

The choice of ends, then, parallels the manner in which we identify ourselves with whatever we recognize as belonging to our "self." This is the theoretical aspect of self-relation that forms the core of subjectivity. In each moment of self-consciousness, we know or feel ourselves to be identical with ourselves; and this knowing or feeling brings into the present (though for the most part only implicitly) everything that we connect with our self. As a result, self-consciousness does have the task, as William James described it, of integrating, in each moment of its experience, all the elements that are a part of its self with the past integrations of the ego that are present through its memory. But this integration is not an action. It is accomplished much more in the feeling of being our self in the present—being everything that we were and will be in the future—in each moment of our self-consciousness. The fact that in self-consciousness the whole of our being is present at every moment may perhaps be appropriately described only as participation in eternity. To clarify this state of affairs more precisely will be our task in the following two chapters.

CHAPTER 4

BEING AND TIME

WHEN SPEAKING of metaphysics, one has to pay attention not only to the tradition of Aristotelian "first philosophy" and its modifications in the Aristotelian scholasticism of the Middle Ages and the philosophy of the Enlightenment. At least in the case of the Greeks, one needs to look also to the history of philosophical thought from its very beginnings, including both Platonists and Stoics, along with the influences stemming from them. When we do this, it appears rather doubtful that metaphysical thought has been so fundamentally determined by the concept of Being as Heidegger claimed. Above all, the distinction of Being itself [*Sein*] from beings [*Seiende*] has scarcely played the decisive role claimed for it in Heidegger's account of the essence and history of metaphysics. The distinction of beings from Being as the *actus essendi* (act of being) appears first to have gained significance for Arabic and Christian philosophers in the Middle Ages. For these thinkers, the separation made it possible to draw an ontological distinction between created beings and the absolute perfection of the Creator, as well as to express the dependence of creatures on the Creator with the help of the concept of Being.

If we look beyond this distinction between Being and

beings for a moment, we can distinguish two different functions of the concept of being in the pre-Aristotelian texts. The first consists in the fact that the word for "a being" is employed as the broadest characterization for all classes of things, and particularly as a starting point for dividing them. Thus Plato (or the Platonic Socrates) can say in the *Phaedo* that there are two classes of beings, namely, what can be seen and the eternal.[1] Aristotle said something similar of the various genera of beings,[2] even though he did not take the concept of being to be the highest genus,[3] since it cannot be fully separated from its particular meanings (e.g., substance, accident, etc.).

The second function of the concept of being is contained in the idea of "real being" [*wahrhaft Seiende*], which had fundamental significance for Plato and can be traced back as far as Parmenides. This term does not have to do with the task of classification, the dividing up of things that proceed from an encompassing whole, but rather with the use of the word "is" in making judgments concerning what is or is not. Plato used the word in this sense in the *Sophist,* when he portrayed the debate of the philosophical schools as a battle of gods and giants, a gigantomachy, regarding being. The debate involved the question whether only corporeal beings exist, or whether the noncorporeal ideas are the real beings while the corporeal things are consigned to becoming and to passing out of existence.[4] The label "real being" implies that it is valid to look beyond that which presents itself as being— namely, that which is perceived by the senses—and to construe it as mere appearance, in order to force one's way through to "real" being.

---

1. Plato *Phaedo* 79a 6-7.
2. Aristotle *Metaphysics* 1004a 5, in *The Complete Works of Aristotle,* 2 vols., ed. Jonathan Barnes (Princeton: Princeton University Press, 1984).
3. Ibid., 998b 22.
4. Plato *Sophist* 246a 4ff.

The Eleatic Stranger of the *Sophist* also interprets the quest of Ionic natural philosophy for a first origin as a quest for real being, because all things that are opposed and plural, to the extent that they share in the fact that they exist, already presuppose being as a more originary unity.[5] This position implies that whatever is accepted as the ultimate origin is at the same time viewed as real being. Further, the comments of the Stranger also link the classificatory function of the concept of being to the question of the ultimate source or principle (*archē*). The implicit reference to the totality of everything that is unified or opposed in the order of the cosmos is nicely expressed in the concept of being, which is the general term for the many that is present in the cosmos. In this manner, the question of the *archē* is incorporated into ontological inquiry. Note, however, that this takes place only when we presuppose a distinction between real being (and unchanging identity) and the realm of becoming and ceasing to exist.

Aristotle corrected Plato's dichotomy between the real being of ideas and the realm of becoming and ceasing to exist. Yet his concepts of form and substance still contain something of this opposition since, ultimately, substance connotes the identical something that lies at the basis of all change. Although Aristotle worked with great care to understand movement and its relation to the essential forms of things, change in his metaphysics remains external to the essential forms themselves.

The idea that real being is immutable became the central target of criticism within process philosophy, as Bergson, Samuel Alexander, and Whitehead turned their critical attention to the metaphysical tradition. For example, Whitehead viewed metaphysics as the striving to provide a conceptual account of the whole of reality. In opposition to Heidegger— who with Nietzsche held metaphysics, but not ontology, to

---

5. Ibid., 243d ff.

be a thing of the past—he proclaimed metaphysics to be unavoidable, while judging its construal as ontology a thing of the past.

One might wish to say that even Whitehead postulated a real being, namely, the elementary events, the "actual entities," out of which all complex and enduring forms are composed. But actual entities are really no longer understood by Whitehead as unchangeable being, since as mere events they are extinguished in the very moment in which they arise; they do not have an enduring character. Nonetheless, a critical examination of Whitehead's atomism reveals that his metaphysical devaluation of enduring forms and entities is just as impossible to maintain as (at the other extreme) the Platonic devaluation of becoming and ceasing to exist in face of the unchangeable, real being of the ideas. No atomistic idea can explain the unity of the many—either in the whole which is the world, or as displayed in the more or less enduring entities and forms—without assuming additional principles. And we must grant such principles at least equal, if not superior, reality.[6] This fact is sufficient reason for rejecting the atomistic thesis that actual entities in their plurality are "the final real things."[7] But, as we can see from Bergson's philosophy, such atomism is certainly not indispensable for making the connection between being and time that process philosophy wishes to achieve. Instead, criticisms of the timelessness of the classical concept of substance are better understood as a final step in the series of developments that began with the

---

6. See my "Atomism, Duration, Form: Difficulties with Process Philosophy," chap. 6 below.

7. Alfred North Whitehead, *Process and Reality: An Essay in Cosmology*, corrected edition, ed. David Ray Griffin and Donald Sherburne (New York: Free Press, 1978), p. 18; 1st American ed. (New York: Macmillan, 1929), p. 27. [Hereafter abbreviated *PR*. Further references will cite the 1st ed. in parentheses.—TRANS.]. At another point Whitehead himself characterizes his system as atomistic: "Thus the ultimate metaphysical truth is atomism" (*PR*, p. 35 [53]).

geometrization of the study of nature in the early period of modern science.

The first result of this development was to make relations independent from substance. As long as one construed relations in an Aristotelian fashion as attributes (as accidents of substance), one had to assume, instead of a single relation between two things, two different relations: that of the first to the second and another of the second to the first. These two relations could not be construed as identical, as is evident from geometrical diagrams. The relational system of space and time was made independent of substances only after the idea of quality had been eliminated, a move brought about by the reduction of secondary qualities to the so-called primary qualities of things, consisting of their geometrical characteristics. In the end, Kant could even construe the category of substance as only a subspecies of relation, since it is meaningful to speak of substances only in relationship to accidents. The "Logic of Essence" developed by Hegel further extended this particular view of the concept of substance.

From that point, it was only a small step to process philosophy. Thinkers began to reflect on the fact that the relations that are determinative for any substance take on concrete form only within the extensive continuum of space-time. Whitehead finally made this explicit in his early writings on the philosophy of natural science. The question then became how the whole of the space-time continuum was to be related to the distinctiveness of the individual events within it. Whitehead and Alexander answered the question in different ways, but both agreed that each individually existing thing is constituted by the totality of the relations in which it stands.

We have viewed process philosophy as the result of the problems raised by the concept of substance as discussed in modern philosophy. The emphasis that process philosophy places on the connection of being and time is further reinforced when we note that another development, proceeding from a very different starting point, converges with its conclusions. What I have in mind is Wilhelm Dilthey's examination of the conditions for historical consciousness. In his *Introduction to the Human Sciences* [*Geisteswissenschaften*] of 1883, Dilthey was concerned in the first place to provide an epistemological foundation for the human sciences and to guarantee their independence from the natural sciences. In his sequel to this book, Dilthey argued that the foundation was to be won by developing a "general psychology" as the basis for giving a psychological interpretation of historical events. But in the course of Dilthey's preparatory work on this theme, the concept of such a general psychology was subtly transformed into a description of the process of the individual's experience, a process that is already constituted by historicity. Bernhard Groethuysen, the editor of the incomplete manuscripts left behind by Dilthey after his death, drew attention to this change. In fact, Dilthey's hermeneutics of historical experience and human self-experience can be compared in several respects to the psychology of William James, whose fundamental concepts were expanded by Whitehead into a general metaphysics.

Dilthey's thought underwent a similar development at the hands of Heidegger. In *Being and Time*, Heidegger referred to the connection between his analysis of the historicity of an individual human existence [*Dasein*] and Dilthey's work.[8] Heidegger was apparently unaware of the texts that Groethuysen had edited and introduced, yet his interpretation stands in actual agreement with the development of Dilthey's thought as documented there. It is clear from Heidegger's comments that, as a matter of fact, not only his section on the historicity of Dasein but the entire conception of *Being and*

---

8. Martin Heidegger, *Being and Time*, trans. J. Macquarrie and E. S. Robinson (New York: Harper & Row, 1962), pp. 449ff. German edition: *Sein und Zeit* (Halle, 1927). [References to the German edition will be given in parentheses.—TRANS.]

Time drew decisive inspiration from Dilthey. In connecting
Dilthey's analysis of historicity with Husserl's program of
general ontology, Heidegger overcame the opposition between the historical and the ontical features of natural events.
Achieving this synthesis allowed Heidegger to utilize the key
insight in Dilthey's analysis of historicity: that the totality of
life, which is never completed within the history of a life,
serves as the basis for the meaning of all individual experiences, and that this meaning therefore changes over the
course of a life history. Heidegger used this insight as the
basis for his new construal of the "meaning of Being" in
general.[9]

However, the connection between being and time, even
as mediated by the not yet completed totality of human
existence, is certainly not as new as Heidegger believed. In
Heidegger's view, the history of the understanding of time
within philosophy had been dominated by the Aristotelian
doctrine of time. This domination, according to *Being and
Time*, "has persisted from Aristotle to Bergson and even
later."[10] The Aristotelian view of time, Heidegger alleges,
works outward counting from the now.[11] The determination
of earlier and later in any given case of "counting" motion
follows directly from this starting point.[12] But Heidegger
does not consider that, for Aristotle, it is the soul that mea-
sures and counts the moments of time, in opposition to Plato,
who derived time from the motion of the heavenly bodies.[13]
The distinction between time and motion forced Aristotle to
have recourse to the soul, though at first only to the extent
that the soul is the locus of counting. The future tense could
then be accounted for only by working out a psychological

---

9. Ibid., p. 455 (403).
10. Ibid., p. 39 (18).
11. Ibid., pp. 473-74 (421-22).
12. Aristotle *Physics* 219b 1ff.
13. Ibid., 223a 25-26; Plato *Timaeus* 38a 7-8.

interpretation of time, a path also followed by Heidegger in developing his own theory of time.

It is important to note that the psychological interpretation of time led thinkers already in the ancient period to analyze time in ways that moved far beyond Aristotle's treatment of the theme. The most significant example of such an analysis is found in Plotinus, who held the position that eternity is the source of time.[14]

Like Aristotle, Plotinus distinguished time from motion, because that which is not moved or remains stationary still remains within time.[15] Yet time and motion, according to Plotinus, cannot be determined by one another in a fully reciprocal fashion, as Aristotle thought, because all measuring already presupposes time.[16] From what source, then, should the essence of time be determined? Following Plato, Plotinus sought to conceive time as the image [Abbild] of eternity. Yet he could not begin, as Plato had done, with any particular form of motion, including circular motion, for time has to be conceived as prior to all motion whatsoever. This is why Plotinus had to develop his theory of time as image by relating it to the totality of the eternal itself. He appealed to the soul for mediation, for while the soul is tied to the eternal, it is also the principle that brings about the moving apart of the various moments of life (the *diastasis . . . zōēs* or "spreading out of life") within the flow of time.[17]

The eternal is the whole of life, namely, of "life that is fixed within Sameness, because the whole is always present in it—not now this, then another, but all simultaneously" in

---

14. See Plotinus, *Enneads*, 6 vols., trans. A. H. Armstrong, Loeb Classical Library (Cambridge: Harvard University Press, 1967), 3.7. See also Werner Beierwaltes, *Plotin über Ewigkeit und Zeit: Enneade III, 7*, 3rd ed. (Frankfurt: Vittorio Klostermann, [1967], 1981).

15. Aristotle *Physics* 219a 1; 221b 10; Plotinus *Enneads* 3.7.8.

16. Cf. Plotinus *Enneads* 3.7.9, 21, 60-61; Aristotle *Physics* 220b 14-16.

17. Plotinus *Enneads* 3.7.11, 41.

the sense of "completion without parts."[18] Because of its participation in the eternal through the Mind or *Nous*, the soul also lives in expectation of its wholeness (and the wholeness of all that is). It "falls from eternity," however, because of its own "desire to control itself" (*archein autēs boulomenēs*).[19] The result is the separation of the moments and parts of life, the *diastasis . . . zōēs*,[20] and along with the independence of the finite or the many, time arises. Time is characterized as the manner in which the many remains bound, even in its independence, to the whole. Given the nature of temporal moments as parts, the whole is present only in the sense that it hovers over the parts as the future whole: "Instead of the completed infinite and whole, [there is only] the moment after moment into the infinite; instead of the unitary whole, [only] the partial and always merely future whole."[21] As a consequence of the decay into parts of the unity of life, the whole becomes only the future goal of all striving within the realm of the finite. The path to this goal is time. In short, when the theory of time is oriented toward the eternal totality, the consequence is a primacy of the future for the understanding of time.[22]

So it was not Heidegger but Plotinus who first maintained the primacy of the future in the understanding of time. Analogously to Heidegger, Plotinus grounded this primacy

---

18. Ibid., 3.7.3 (p. 303): "a partless completion" (*telos amerēs*). See Beierwaltes's commentary on this passage, *Plotin*, pp. 162-68.

19. Plotinus *Enneads* 3.7.11, 15.

20. Ibid., 41.

21. Ibid., 7, 11 (p. 343): *anti de apeirou ēdē kai olou to eis apeiron pros to ephexēs aei, anti de athroou olou to kata meros esomenon kai aei esomenon olon.* Armstrong translates the passage: "and instead of a complete unbounded whole, a continuous unbounded succession, and instead of a whole all together, a whole which is, and always will be, going to come into being part by part" (p. 343). See Beierwaltes's commentary, *Plotin*, pp. 171ff.

22. See Beierwaltes, *Plotin*, pp. 272-73; cf. pp. 65ff.

in the fact that the totality of existence is possible only from the standpoint of its future. Of course, for Plotinus, the totality that we presuppose in order to comprehend time implies that eternity is to be understood as the form of being of the divine. Similarly, the soul of which Plotinus speaks is not in the first place the individual human soul, but the world soul. By contrast, Heidegger is concerned with the possibility of attaining wholeness for a finite, individual existence [*Dasein*]. In between these two central notions lies the Christian adaptation of Plotinus's doctrine of time in Augustine and the secularization of this adaptation by Kant.

Augustine, after some hesitation, rejected the supposition of a world soul, limiting his reflection concerning the relationship of time and soul to the individual human soul. For him, the formation of finite things and of individual souls was not the result of some fall of the world soul from its unity with the Logos, but rather the product of the divine act of creation. For this reason, when Augustine linked time to the soul, he was trying to establish not the source of time (say, by construing the soul as proceeding out of eternity), but rather the participation of the soul in eternity—despite its transitory nature and its location within the created world. But, in contrast to Plotinus, Augustine does not view the participation of the soul in the eternal from the standpoint of its future wholeness, despite the fact that he could have appealed to numerous connections with biblical eschatology. The great treatment of time in the eleventh book of the *Confessions* instead focuses attention on the notion of a time-bridging present within the life of the soul.

With this move, Augustine advances beyond Plotinus to an independent analysis of the *experience* of time, one that has remained definitive for all later treatments of the human consciousness of time. The act of experiencing the present is not limited to the moment of the now, which divorces past from future and is itself already past at the moment we notice it. More accurately, one can say that, to a certain extent, we hold ourselves in the present through the *memoria* of the past and the *expectatio* of the future. For Augustine, the central examples of this sort of time-bridging present are to be found in the understanding of spoken discourse and in listening to music. Spoken discourse is articulated within the flow of time; nonetheless, we grasp it as a whole when we comprehend the unity of a sentence. Likewise, a song can be heard and sung only insofar as the whole of the song is already present to me before it begins, and insofar as what has already sounded remains in my memory.[23]

At the basis of the act of experiencing a time-bridging present lies an "extension" of the soul beyond the momentary now (*distentio animi*).[24] The unity of the time-bridging present is effected by means of attention (*attentio*), which is directed toward what has been and what will be.[25] To the extent that attention can pull together that which is separated within time, and which advances moment by moment, into the unity

---

23. Augustine, *The Confessions of St. Augustine*, trans. E. B. Pusey, Everyman Philosophy and Theology, vol. 200a (New York: E. P. Dutton, 1951), 11.28.38.

24. Ibid., 11.26.33. *Distentio* means, on the one hand, "extension," as in this passage and also at 11.23.30. But it can also carry the meaning of "distention," as in 11.29.39, according to which human life has fallen into distention (*distentio est vita mea*) and requires collection into the One: "not distended but *extended* . . . not distractedly but intently, *I follow on for the prize of my heavenly calling*" (*non distentus, sed extentus, non secundum distentionem, sed secundum intentionem sequor ad palmam supernae vocationis*). See also 11.31.41, where Augustine says of God that he has made heaven and earth "without any distraction of Thy action" (*sine distentione actionis tuae*). G. O'Daly has argued that "distention" alone is the definitive meaning; see his "Time as *Distentio* and St. Augustine's Exegesis of Phil. 3,12-14," *Revue Etudes Augustiniennes* 23 (1977): 267-71. For a criticism of this position, see E. A. Schmidt, *Zeit und Geschichte bei Augustin* (Heidelberg: SHAW, 1985), p. 23 n. 36. According to Schmidt, the formula does not stem from a specific philosophical school, but rather had "long since become a readily available formula within the teaching activity of rhetoric."

25. Augustine *Confessions* 11.28.38.

of *one particular* present, we experience duration, the *spatium temporis*.[26] Duration is a picture or image of eternity, a (however limited) sense of and participation in eternity. Interestingly, the young Augustine, in his essay on music, characterized the movement of the heavens, which according to Plato's *Timaeus* is an imitation of eternity, as a "song of the universe" *(carmen universitatis)*.[27] This song, the music of the spheres, consists in the series of temporal events which is ordered in accord with the relations between numbers. Time as duration is therefore to be found not only within the human soul—even though Augustine occasionally expresses himself in this way—but in every ordered series.[28] Nonetheless, time

---

26. Cf. Schmidt, *Zeit und Geschichte*, pp. 28ff. In *Confessions* 11.23.30 Augustine at first speaks of a "space of time" *(spatium temporis)* in the sense of the objective temporal unit of the day. Yet he develops this position in such a manner that the "space of time" appears problematic, since the present as such has no extension *(spatium, 11.27.34)*. Nonetheless, the spoken word "tends" toward a time-bridging present, in which it can be grasped as a unity (ibid.). Augustine ultimately identifies the basis for this in the attention or consideration (11.28.37: *perdurat attentio*). Through the mediation of *memoria* and *expectatio*—the latter, according to Schmidt (pp. 33ff.), being grounded in *memoria*— the past and future are present to the *attentio:* "but 'consideration' is present with me, that through it what was future may be conveyed over, so as to become past" *(praesens tamen adest attentio mea, per quam traiciatur quod erat futurum ut fiat praeteritum, 11.28.38)*. According to Schmidt (p. 30), Augustine recognized this phenomenon as the "imperfect present" *(praesens imperfectum)* within grammar. Augustine attributes to the present understood as attention *(praesens attentio)*—in contrast to the present understood as an extensionless point—the quality of duration (and therefore also of extension), in the sense of a time-bridging present. Augustine's view contrasts with the position of Schmidt (p. 28), who has in view only the pointlike *praesens*, which indeed has no extension.

27. Augustine *De musica* 6.11.

28. See Augustine *Confessions* 11.28.37; cf. 23.30 on sun, day, and time. Schmidt *(Zeit und Geschichte,* pp. 54ff.) notes correctly that Augustine also acknowledges a "time of the creatures" which is independent of the human soul. Unfortunately, he does not enter into the

is *experienced* only within the soul on account of the *distentio animi*.

The connection of the Augustinian *distentio animi* with Plotinus's characterization of time as *diastasis zōēs* has been frequently noted.[29] The connection may have been mediated through Basil, as J. F. Callahan has argued.[30] But, whereas Plotinus focuses on the separation of the moments of life within time, Augustine brings about a positive revaluation by means of his notion of the faculty of attention that bridges temporal moments: The extension of the soul works precisely to synthesize what has been separated in the series of temporal moments. With this move, Augustine establishes the idea of time as duration, even though he does not yet use the expression *duratio* in this context.[31] The view of duration as the synthesis of what is separated within the flow of time is significant from a metaphysical as well as a psychological perspective, for it can also be applied to creatures other than human beings. The being of all finite things is of course closely tied to their duration. All finite being is grounded in

---

problem of how the unity of such temporal units, *tempora*, is finally to be established, given that time as such lacks duration. This problem emerges already in *Confessions* 11.23.30. Augustine is able to solve it for the human experience of time by means of the time-bridging *attentio*, which links memory and expectation together. But he cannot solve it for the cosmic units of time, since he both rejects the identification of time with motion (e.g., with the sun as the basis for the unity of the day, 11.24.31) and no longer has the possibility (after turning his back on the belief in a world soul) of using his insights into the soul as the standard of time for understanding the cosmic "times."

29. Cf. Beierwaltes, *Plotin*, pp. 265ff. Even if Augustine has here simply made use of rhetorical pedagogical knowledge which was no longer influenced by a particular philosophical school (so Schmidt; see n. 24 above), the question of the conceptual relationship with Plotinus's position remains.

30. Basil *Adversus Eunomius* 1.21.

31. Still, he comes close to doing so: "and yet our consideration continueth" (*perdurat attentio,* 11.28.37).

81

its limited participation in the divine eternity, an eternity that was understood as identical with the being and life of God as early as in Plotinus's philosophy.

One finds in Augustine, admittedly, only preliminary suggestions in this direction. In his comments on the being of creatures, Augustine limited himself primarily to the viewpoint of their dependence upon God's creative will; the temporality of created being as such is not elaborated further. In particular, Augustine does not utilize the future, as Plotinus did, in its significant role for interpreting the being of creatures as being whole. In the *Confessions*, *memoria* and *expectatio* stand next to each other as if on the same level, as indications of the extension of the soul in both temporal directions. Augustine really ought to have affirmed the primacy of the future, given his concern with establishing the totality of the being that makes its appearance within temporal duration. In this respect, Augustine's work remains inferior to the analysis provided by Plotinus.[32] Only Heidegger again advanced the primacy of the future for the understanding of time, albeit in a much reduced form compared to Plotinus and Augustine. The reduction consists precisely in the loss of any connection, within the analysis of time, to the idea of eternity.

This reduction is already characteristic of Kant's analysis of time in the *Critique of Pure Reason*. The unity of time—

---

32. So also Schmidt, *Zeit und Geschichte*, pp. 49-50; cf. p. 38. Schmidt traces this conclusion back to Augustine's view of time as a creature, which as such stands in contrast to the divine eternity (pp. 50-51). Yet this difference need not necessarily exclude a striving of the creatures for fellowship with God as their *summum bonum*, an idea which could be utilized for our understanding of time.

From another perspective, Augustine's view of the creatureliness of time (in contrast to Plotinus's derivation of time from a "fall" of the soul) makes possible a fundamentally positive evaluation of time. Augustine begins to employ this positive view in his notion of the "times" that are determined by the Creator with their established durations, although he only partially develops this thought.

which Kant also took as the condition for comprehending the limited moments of time—is no longer provided by the unity of eternity, but by the unity of the ego. Time is, for Kant, "the form . . . of the intuition of ourselves and of our inner state," specifically, that having to do with "the relation of representations in our inner state."[33] In the second edition of the *Critique of Pure Reason* (1787), Kant elucidated this thesis by postulating that the ego might be "affected by itself."[34] Through "its own activity" in positing its representations, the mind is affected by intuitions, which grasp the unity of time in three relationships: temporal succession, simultaneity, and endurance through temporal change.

Kant here attempts to derive the unity of time in intuition from the unity of the ego. However, we must raise objections to this project similar to those already raised against the transcendental-subjective interpretation of spatial intuition in Kant's work. Just as space as the infinite whole precedes the comprehension of all partial spaces and spatial objects, so also, according to Kant, time is given in intuition as an infinite whole.[35] Yet the ego is not an infinite whole. Consequently, the awareness of time cannot be based upon the self-intuition of the ego. Instead, we must conclude, with Descartes, that the concept of the ego is itself possible only as a limitation of the Infinite; the idea of the ego already presupposes an intuition of the Infinite that lies at the basis of the forms of intuition (space and time). Space and time must then already be viewed as specific forms of this primordial intuition of the Infinite. If in the process, as Kant thought, priority is ascribed to time as the "inner sense," perhaps we can understand the difference of the various temporal moments by means of the experience of the self in consciousness; still, there is no way to understand the unity of these moments through the unity of time. To grasp

---

33. Kant, *Critique of Pure Reason*, A 33.
34. Ibid., B 67-68.
35. Ibid., B 48; cf. B 39-40.

this unity, we must have recourse to an infinite unity that rises above subjectivity. The result is that Plotinus's derivation of time from eternity is conceptually superior to Kant's attempt to reduce everything to the transcendental subject.

The same thing is true of Heidegger's analysis of time in *Being and Time.* Kant replaces eternity, as the horizon for time, with the subjectivity of the ego; Heidegger replaces it with individual human existence [*Dasein*]. The primacy of the future rests for Heidegger upon the anticipation of or "running forward" to [*Vorlaufen*] the ultimate possibility of Dasein: one's own death. The possibility of Dasein's becoming whole is grounded in that source.[36] In view of the future which is one's own death, the future appears as "the coming [*Kunft*], in which Dasein, in its ownmost potentiality-for-Being, comes toward itself."[37]

Now Heidegger does not presuppose, as Kant does, an ego that is always already identical with itself as the locus of temporal awareness. Rather, the identity of Dasein is supposed to be constituted first of all by the future, in such a manner that Dasein, from the future of its own death, is disclosed as a whole in its finitude and can appropriate itself as the "ownmost having-been." Still, the totality of Dasein is neither located in eternity nor derived through participation in eternity, as was the case for Plotinus and Augustine, but stems from the finitude of Dasein as such. For Heidegger, the key is this "running forward," this act of anticipating one's own death as the seal of finitude. The other side of human existence is our thrownness, the contingency of the There [*des Da*]. Running forward to the most extreme possibility of our own death enables us to "appropriate our thrownness" as the form of our having-been.[38]

---

36. Martin Heidegger, *Being and Time,* pp. 356ff.; cf. pp. 279-80, 285ff. (309-10; cf. 236-37, 241ff.).

37. Ibid., p. 373 (325).

38. Ibid., pp. 372ff. (325-26).

At first glance, Heidegger's analysis may remind one of Augustine. Augustine's "extension of the soul" [*distentio animi*] links together memory and expectation in the unity of duration by means of the time-bridging *attentio*, just as Heidegger links future and past within the authentic present in which Dasein is present to itself.[39] Yet, while Augustine's *distentio animi*, united by *attentio*, rests on a (however limited) participation in the divine eternity, in which everything that is separate within the flow of time is present within a single eternal moment, Heidegger emphatically stresses that Dasein is finite precisely in its temporality. Decisive for Heidegger's view is the finitude of the future itself: the authentic future, out of which Dasein originally makes itself temporal, is, according to him, experienced only through the anticipation of one's own death. Any critical treatment of Heidegger's analysis of time must begin with this particular claim.

Does knowledge of our own death really provide the basic context for comprehending our experience of the future and hence our consciousness of time as a whole? The plausibility of this thesis depends upon the assumption that the knowledge of one's own death discloses the whole of Dasein as a finite being. And lying behind this assumption, in turn, is Dilthey's claim that the relativity of experienced meaning, which changes constantly in the course of historical experience, comes to rest only in the hour of death: "Only in the final moment of a life can an estimate be made concerning its significance. . . . One would have to wait for the end of a life and survey the whole in the hour of death. Only from there could one ascertain the relation of its parts."[40] According to

---

39. Ibid., p. 376 (328).

40. Wilhelm Dilthey, *Gesammelte Schriften*, 16 vols. in 18, ed. Bernhard Groethuysen (Leipzig: Tübner, and Göttingen: Vandenhoeck & Ruprecht, 1914-72), 7:237, 233. Nonetheless, Dilthey, in contrast to Heidegger, saw the embeddedness of the individual life within more encompassing historical life-contexts. Thus he continued: "one would have to wait for the end of history in order to possess complete material

Heidegger, the totality of Dasein is already available at an earlier point, because it belongs to human existence to know of one's death. By "running forward," then, the possibility of being whole can be anticipated. Still, for Heidegger as for Dilthey, the possibility that Dasein in its finitude might become whole continues to depend upon death.

But it is precisely at this point that we must ask whether an individual human existence [*Dasein*] is actually made into a totality through its death. Is not an existence much more broken up, fragmented, by death? Does not the possible totality of an existence always extend beyond whatever death makes of it? Sartre rejected Heidegger's thesis on the basis of such questions. We will need another light than the one that death throws on a life, if we are to recognize in that life some sort of totality. An expression of this fact can be found in the convictions and hopes of various peoples that they will experience some future beyond death.

If death is not able to make an individual human existence into a totality, we must also reject the thesis that death has a constitutive significance for the experience of time. Even so, this does not affect the manner in which, in human existence, future and possible wholeness belong together, nor the primacy of the future for the experience of time that Plotinus defended. If there are serious problems with any attempt to make finitude independent of the Infinite—in the manner pursued by Heidegger and, before him, by Kant— then analysis of time must be bound together with the concept of eternity, as in the thought of Plotinus. The possible wholeness of human existence can then be construed only as participation in eternity. At the same time, however, it must be understood as the wholeness of a *finite* being, in contrast

---

for determining the meaning of history" (p. 233). The "meaning-whole" of the individual life cannot be completely separated from society and history.

to Plotinus, who focused his thought on the world soul rather than on the individual soul.

The finitude of human existence entails the distinction of future from present and past, because duration as the time-bridging present is never able to grasp and maintain in itself the whole of human existence. Thus, peculiar to the future is the ambivalence of possible completion on the one side and of possible failure and destruction on the other. This ambivalence is constitutive for the contingency of all those events that are a part of human existence as we experience it, and at least co-constitutive for the contingency of human existence in its very finitude. Nonetheless, the leading role in our consciousness of time belongs to the future understood as the source of possible completion, as can be clearly seen in Plotinus. Working outward from this perspective, the present and the past can then be interpreted as participating in the future totality, or as falling short of it.

With this last sentence, our discussion of time returns once again to the theme of being, although this theme has of course been implicit throughout our discussion of time. The question of the wholeness of Dasein in Heidegger always involves its identity, its "what it is," its essence as a unitary being even as it is extended through time. Since Parmenides, wholeness and essence have belonged together. As long as the future is the source of the possible wholeness of an individual human existence, then we must say that its essence, and thus its "what it is," are determined by its future. In the same way, Dilthey makes the significance of life as a whole (which is the framework for meaning that he chooses) dependent upon its temporal end. This implies that the essence of life as a whole is temporal; it depends upon whatever future it is whose coming will bring about the wholeness of this whole. When Heidegger, moving beyond Dilthey's analyses of historicity, maintains that the possibility of being whole lies for Dasein in the anticipation of its death, he thereby implies that Dasein exists in the mode of anticipation.

Yet Heidegger did not present his analytic of Dasein simply for its own sake; he treated it as the point of access and the key to a general ontology. This, however, raises the question whether beings are to be conceived in general as the anticipation of their essences. This conception would mean that *everything* that exists is what it is only as the anticipation of its future, in which (along with its finitude) the wholeness of each being might be established. In the course of time, as long as something is, its end remains before it; still, it is what it is always in anticipation of its end and from its end.

Such a view of the connection between being and time remains unaffected by the criticisms that we raised regarding Heidegger's position in *Being and Time*. It may be that the primacy of the future for Dasein's temporality—and for beings in general—cannot be appropriately grasped from the standpoint of death (or, more generally, from the standpoint of nothingness), that the totality of each being, despite its finitude, can only be conceived through its participation in eternity. Nonetheless, it may still be the case that the future is to be construed as the source of the wholeness of finite being, and its being as the anticipation of its future.

Three conclusions follow. The presence of being as duration, when understood along the lines of the Augustinian "extension of the soul" [*distentio animi*], appears as a limited participation in eternity. As the future of finite beings, eternity represents simultaneously the possibility that they will be completed and that they will end; in this ambivalence it is also the contingent source of their being. The past appears as the limit of participation in eternity in the other direction, for finite beings are not able to make present to themselves both their own being and the being of the world to which they have been connected. This inability belongs to the imperfection of their being, as well as to their finitude, which is not, as such, imperfection.

Finally, the passage of time appears as a series of temporal moments, each of which—days, weeks, years—is participation in eternity and all of which are tied together again by memory and expectation into a unity. This unity is admittedly no longer a unity of experiencing but instead the unity of a trained [*gebildeten*] consciousness. Nevertheless, it is now able to rise above the difference of one's own being from other finite beings and from the Infinite. This unity is therefore—though in another fashion, now through the medium of thought—a participation in the eternal to an even greater extent than the unmediated, time-bridging unity of experiencing.[41]

In the next chapter, when we discuss the idea of anticipation, we will have to consider what consequences these conclusions have for our understanding of the identity of being and for a new approach to the concept of substance. Let me just mention in closing one possible consequence of our discussion for the understanding of space-time, that is, the connection of time and space. Interacting critically with Bergson's arguments against the spatialization of time, Samuel Alexander interpreted the space-time connection as involving the claim that time owes its very continuity to its connection with space. Without space, time would be only a series of discontinuous moments. The series attains continuity, according to Alexander, only through the fact that the temporal

---

41. According to E. Pöppel, the "upper temporal boundary" for the "integration of events that are temporally separated in perceived shapes—which as such are always 'now,' that is, present," is roughly two to four seconds. See his "Erlebte Zeit und die Zeit überhaupt: Ein Versuch der Integration," in *Die Zeit, Schriften der Carl-Friedrich-von-Siemens-Stiftung* (Munich, Vienna, 1983), pp. 369-82 (quote from p. 372). Pöppel argues that extension reaches much further in the experience of duration, which is dependent "on manipulated information" (pp. 373ff.). But Pöppel's theses on "time in general," which go beyond these findings, provide an informative example of what happens when one ignores the fact that empirical-scientific results not only provide a foundation for philosophical reflection but also, in their conceptual framework, already imply the results of such reflection.

moments that follow one upon another take place at the same location.[42] But we have shown that the flow of temporal moments cannot be conceived at all without presupposing, with Plotinus, the eternal simultaneity of all that is separated within time. Hence, even within the finite experience of time, the necessity of presupposing a future completion is evidence that there is an anticipation of completion whenever what is not simultaneous is made simultaneous, as occurs in the phenomenon of duration. This sort of simultaneity provides an adequate basis for establishing the simultaneity of things that are separated in space. At any rate, on this view space is not required for an understanding of the continuity of time. Instead, we are able to account for both forms of simultaneity (that of duration and that of the intuition of space), as well as the spatialized thought that Bergson judged so harshly.[43] Each of these can now be understood as involving some type of participation in the interrelatedness of everything divided by time at the moment of eternity.

---

42. Samuel Alexander, *Space, Time and Deity* (New York: Macmillan, [1920], 1966), 1:48-49, 143; cf. p. 149.

43. Henri Bergson derived the consciousness of space from that of time by means of counting temporal units (*Time and Free Will*, pp. 78ff. [=*Essai*, pp. 54ff. (1889 ed., pp. 59ff.)]). Space is already given with this counting. This is not the case in the experience of pure duration, according to Bergson. Like Augustine, he illustrates this with the example of listening to a melody (ibid., pp. 86-87, 100-101): pure duration is linked with a feeling of flow but without the separation and counting of successive moments. This analysis, however, leaves out the very thing Augustine sought to present using the same example: the time-bridging present as participating in eternity. If indeed the time-bridging present is understood in this Augustinian sense, then the "spatialization" of the succession of time is seen in a more positive light than is the case in Bergson. The idea of space as the expression of simultaneity in the time-bridging present is itself then to be conceived as a form of participation in the eternal simultaneity of eternity.

CHAPTER 5

CONCEPT AND ANTICIPATION

TRADITIONAL METAPHYSICAL reflection was characterized by the domination of the concept and by reflection that was focused on the quest for logical necessity. So, at any rate, runs the diagnosis of two of the most reflective critics of metaphysics, Wilhelm Dilthey and Martin Heidegger. These thinkers had in mind the domination of the concept and of logic when they proclaimed the end of metaphysics.

The sort of metaphysics that Dilthey believed could no longer be continued confronted him in the guise of Hegel's system. Yet Dilthey viewed Hegel's Logic of the Concept not as an unforeseen development within the history of philosophy but as the consistent unfolding of the starting point formulated in Leibniz's Principle of Sufficient Reason and traceable back as far as Descartes's demand for clear and distinct ideas. Dilthey insisted that not only modern metaphysics had been ruled by foundationalist thinking; the roots of its domination run all the way back to the Greek origins of metaphysics. There thinkers were concerned with the inquiry into the "ultimate grounds" of everything that is.[1] Since the time of Plato and Aristotle, this question had been addressed

---

1. Wilhelm Dilthey, *Gesammelte Schriften*, 1:133.

by means of a "philosophy of the concept,"[2] at first in the guise of a "metaphysics of substantial forms," as it was developed by Plato himself, and later along different lines by Aristotle.

The domination of the concept in metaphysical thought—what Dilthey called "logicism"—was the basis for the fact that, despite the convergence between philosophical and biblical monotheism, the historical relationship between metaphysics and Christian theology again and again had the appearance of a conflict in principle. Until the beginnings of the modern age, theology had been primarily interested in preventing the rise of any such conflict in principle between faith and reason. In Christian reflection during the Middle Ages, by contrast, Averroism had defended the self-sufficiency of philosophy, even to the extent of admitting direct conflict, thereby anticipating the emancipation of modern philosophy from theological tutelage. Modern philosophy then rose up against theology, advocating rational universality, narrowing the responsibilities of religion and theology to the leftover needs of subjectivity, and finally claiming to bring even these to conceptual expression. Since that time, theology—at least where it did not cut out a scholastic philosophy tailored to its own needs and seek to keep it alive by artificial means, as occurred in the Catholic tradition—has resorted increasingly to distance, working to isolate its own themes from philosophy.

The claim to transcend-yet-preserve [*Aufhebung*] religion or religious representations within the realm of the concept, paradigmatically expressed in Hegel's system, is thus only the symptom of a more general lack. This lack does not merely concern the relationship of philosophy to religion and theology; it is the symptom of disregarding the finitude of philosophical thought, or at least of neglecting the significance of this fact for the form taken by philosophical reflection. Kierkegaard accused Hegel of precisely this disregard,

---

2. Ibid., p. 184.

and Dilthey's critique of metaphysics boils down to basically the same point.

Any renewal of metaphysics that wishes to rise above such objections must give adequate place to human finitude, the finitude that results from the historicity of every starting point for metaphysical reflection. Of course, this does not exclude the Infinite and Absolute (and, closely tied to this, the whole of reality itself) from being a possible object of philosophical reflection. Hegel was right in insisting that the idea of the Infinite is always thought along with the idea of finitude. Nevertheless, it is true for the ideas of the Infinite and Absolute, as it is for the formulation of any principles pertaining to all being and knowledge, that they remain bound to a particular set of finite conditions for philosophical reflection. In fact, Hegel's logic concentrated on precisely these conditions; it emphasized reflection on the finitude of all philosophical determinations of the Absolute to the point of making this finitude the methodological foundation for its dialectical development.

The question is: Has Hegel's Absolute Idea, as the concept that has attained full realization, been able to transcend the boundaries of finitude? To doubt such claims, one need not construe finitude and its limits as themselves absolute, nor need one forbid philosophy from reflecting on the Infinite and Absolute. Quite the opposite: such doubt can only lead to a greater degree of rational clarity concerning the place of reflection within "conscious life." Philosophical reflection, when understood in Dieter Henrich's sense, can seek to clarify the obscurities within experiential knowledge—and this includes the obscurities of religious representations as well. Nonetheless, when one pursues this task, one cannot let the philosophical concept transcend its own starting point in experiential knowledge, a limitation that applies equally to the religious consciousness.

The implication is clear: Any metaphysics, if it is to be taken seriously, can no longer claim the character of a definitive foundation, constructed of concepts, for being and knowledge. Metaphysical reflection must instead take on the form of a *conjectural reconstruction* in relation to its object, one which distinguishes itself from its intended truth while at the same time construing itself as a preliminary form of this truth. Its characteristic reflective form will thus have to be more that of anticipation than that of concept in the sense of classical metaphysics. Put more precisely, the philosophical concept will reveal itself to have the structure of anticipation.

The exact sciences present us with examples of reflection that proceeds by means of anticipation, to the extent that scientists occupy themselves with the formation of hypotheses and with their testing. This process does not have to do with the anticipations of perception attributed by Kant to the a priori structure of the understanding. Kant's anticipations were linked to "the pure determinations in space and time, in respect of shape as well as of magnitude,"[3] especially to the substratum and extent of the impressions. But hypothetical thought is more accurately anticipatory in the sense that it reaches out toward or anticipates [*vorgreift*] empirical constellations by means of assertions, which then require confirmation or refutation through experience.

In the same way, every assertion has an anticipatory structure. For its truth claim can be called into doubt and discussed, implying that whatever truth it claims is not yet definitive or indubitably settled. Even metaphysical assertions are to be viewed in this sense as hypothetical and anticipatory, namely, as hypotheses that are directed toward reality as a whole: "world hypotheses," as Stephen Pepper called them. Now it may well be that metaphysical assertions have a hypothetical function in this sense. But metaphysical reflection is above all directed toward the *structure* of anticipations and toward their understanding of truth, for it cannot remain at the level of a simple opposition between assertion

---

3. Kant, *Critique of Pure Reason,* B 209.

and reality—especially since world hypotheses in Pepper's sense cannot be evaluated merely on the basis of individual empirical observations.

Anticipations look forward, on the one hand, to the occurrence of future experience and, on the other, to the content of such experience. But this phenomenon raises a question: does not the anticipation remain external to the content toward which it is directed, simply because of the temporal difference between the anticipation and the anticipated experience? Such externality would be the case if the content were provided only upon the advent of the corresponding experience. In that case, anticipation would not be a form appropriate to its own content.

In the light of this difficult question, the discussion of the concept of anticipation within theology may be of philosophical interest.[4] Within Protestant theology, especially since the portrayal of Jesus' message by Johannes Weiss (1892) and particularly in the last three decades, the concept of anticipation has been employed to describe the relationship between Jesus' message concerning the coming kingdom of God and the future of this coming itself. Derivatively, it has also been used to describe the relationship between the resurrection of Jesus and a future general resurrection of the dead, as is awaited in Jewish apocalyptic. The structural parallel between Jesus' message of the kingdom of God and the event of his resurrection from the dead is remarkable: in both cases the future—in the one case, of the kingdom of God; in the other, of the eschatological resurrection of the dead—is viewed as already and actually having broken into history. The final reality is present: in the case of the resurrection of Jesus, this reality has a continuing effect through the presence of the Spirit of life, for the resurrection of Jesus himself is believed

---

4. See Lothar Kugelmann, *Antizipation. Eine begriffsgeschichtliche Untersuchung* (Göttingen: Vandenhoeck & Ruprecht, 1986), esp. pp. 23-56.

to be the Spirit's creative work. And still, the future that will reveal the truth about the present remains open and ahead of us. Without the definitive coming of the kingdom of God, the message of Jesus—along with the demand to subordinate all else to this future coming—remains a matter of religious enthusiasm. Of particular embarrassment will be Jesus' proclamation that the future of the kingdom of God has already become present in his works and for those who respond in faith to his message. The truth of this anticipation hinges on the still-absent future. Only if that future actually arrives was it in fact already present in the life of Jesus.

Similar conclusions apply to the early Christian Easter message. The proclamation of Jesus' resurrection presupposes the future resurrection of the dead. In a world in which dead persons turn out not to rise again someday, the Christian Easter message is exposed to overwhelming doubt. But from the perspective of a future general resurrection, the resurrection of Jesus will appear not only as real but also as the anticipatory realization of this final completion, corresponding to the presence of the kingdom of God in Jesus' own message. Judged from the perspective of eschatology, this anticipation takes on the character of an incarnation of God himself in the person of Jesus.

Here we find anticipation to be a real instance of something's occurring in advance. The anticipated future is already present in its anticipation—though only given the presupposition that the eschatological future of God's Lordship and the resurrection of the dead actually occur. If this future does not occur, then its anticipation will have been only prophetic enthusiasm. Anticipation is therefore always ambiguous; its true significance depends upon the future course of experience.

This insight holds quite generally. The anticipating consciousness as such does not guarantee the truth of its content. Of course, the christological model cannot be generalized in every respect. The message of Jesus and his resurrection have to do with final salvation. By comparison, every other form of anticipation can have only preliminary meaning, one which leaves open the ultimate truth concerning humankind. But since, according to Christian doctrine, God as Creator is already related to each of his creatures in love, all created life is to be understood as a form of participation in the divine eternity, however weak or limited this participation may be. The length of time granted to each creature can then be interpreted as an anticipation of the final completion that is expected from the future of God's rule. At that time, the creatures, despite their finitude, will participate in the eternity of God, at least to the extent that they do not close themselves off from that eternity.

That finite, time-bound beings can only expect to participate in eternity from the future is a conclusion that can be derived from Plotinus's doctrine of time and eternity. On this point, Plotinus's thought is just as compatible with the eschatological orientation of biblical thought as that of his master, Plato. Plato held that the ideas (as principles of the Good) could be realized only by striving after the Good and could be allotted to things only as their future. But it remained unclear [within the Platonic tradition] how *present* life could be understood as a real participation in this future Good, as a real anticipation of eternity. To see how this was to be done, one has to turn to Augustine, whose development of the idea of duration as time-bridging present effectively advanced our understanding of the question.

We now begin to see the broader context for the treatment of being and time which I began in the previous chapter. Already there, we found that Augustine's reflections led us in the direction of the concept of anticipation, although he himself did not explicitly use this term. In fact, he did not even come close to it, because he chose not to appropriate Plotinus's connection between eternity and the future. Participation in eternity by means of a time-bridging present, according to Augustine, takes place vertically, through a relation of imaging [*Abbild*]; it is not mediated by any reference to the future. At this point, we see a limitation of Augustine's Platonic-Christian synthesis: although he conceived of God in good Platonic fashion as the highest human Good, he did not thematize the reference to the future that this move implies nor link it to biblical eschatology. Augustine thus failed to make use of a potentially fruitful aspect of Platonic thought for Christian theology. How well he might have been able to tie together the theology of history and the doctrine of God, from the viewpoint of the futurity of the Good! But he did not do it. His doctrine that God is the highest Good therefore retained a hint of the rejection of the world typical of the late ancient period, and the participation in eternity remained bound up with the motif of timelessness.

For one other theologian of the early Church the concept of anticipation also played an important role, in this case, in interpreting the concept of faith.[5] Clement of Alexandria, a good century and a half before Augustine, interpreted faith as the anticipation or *prolepsis* of future salvation. In doing so, he followed a terminological convention that went back to the epistemology of Epicurus. The Stoics had modified this convention into the assumption that particular concepts, such as the concept of God and the knowledge of ethical obligations, were built into human nature. Such concepts are only fleshed out in the process of experience; still, they are anticipated or "taken in advance" before a person develops the ability to analyze and to justify conceptually.

By interpreting faith as prolepsis, Clement characterized it as a knowledge that is already present before its final confirmation at the eschatological completion, namely, through anticipation. Faith and knowledge could thereby be seen as parallel in their structure, because the concept of anticipation brought the element of time into play in the

---

5. In this regard, see Kugelmann's comments, ibid., pp. 121-25. On the anticipation concept of Epicurus and the Stoics, see pp. 110ff.

understanding of knowledge itself. It was not until the discovery of the historicity of experiential knowledge that a similar methodological framework was again provided. In the light of the historicity of experience, *all* consciousness of meaning is revealed as changeable, and every claim to knowledge as an anticipation of some future confirmation.

The category of anticipation does not arise simply as an alternative to the category of the concept. At least this is true as long as by "concept" we mean the act of conceiving some designated thing and not merely an arbitrarily stipulated term. When we focus on concepts which are appropriate or which intend a given thing, construing them as anticipations simply draws explicit attention to a structural component that otherwise remains hidden: the dependence of the concept upon verification through the thing that it grasps, a verification that as such transcends the mere concept. Characterizing concepts as anticipations therefore does not imply an abandonment of rationality, but rather intends to do more justice to rationality, in comparison with descriptions that conflate the true concept of a thing and the thing itself.

At one point, Kant affirmed the anticipatory essence of the concepts of the understanding—and, in particular, of the a priori concepts of the understanding—without exploring in detail the implications of this fact.[6] Looking back over the "Transcendental Analytic," in the section of the *Critique of Pure Reason* concerning phenomena and noumena, Kant characterizes as the "important result" of the "Transcendental Analytic" "that the understanding can never accomplish more a priori than to anticipate the form of possible experience in general."[7] Correspondingly, we read at the begin-

---

6. Kant, *Critique of Pure Reason*, B 303. Kugelmann explores in detail the relationship of this comprehensively formulated statement to the more specific problematic of the "anticipations of perception" (*Antizipation*, pp. 90-110).

7. Kant, *Critique of Pure Reason*, A 246.

ning of the section concerning anticipations of perception: "one can label as an anticipation each item of knowledge through which I can know and determine a priori that which belongs to empirical knowledge."[8]

These are certainly very fundamental (albeit neither further established nor developed) statements concerning the apriority that Kant claims for the functions of the understanding as well as for the forms of intuition. Yet, as is well known, Kant writes at another point that the understanding dictates to nature its laws. How is this latter claim related to the function of anticipation? The prolepseis of Epicurus and the Stoics, which Kant here recalls,[9] were certainly not independent of all experience; they revealed themselves as anticipations precisely through the fact that they were confirmed in the further course of experience. In the case of Stoic thought, proleptic assertions even received their precise form via the process of experience. At any rate, there is within the structure of anticipation a dependence of the validity claims upon what is anticipated. Kant did not thematize this dependence in the case of the a priori forms, any more than he thematized the temporal structure of anticipation. Yet this temporal structure brings clearly to view the dependence of the anticipated concept upon the thing to which it refers.

Another aspect of Kant's comments concerning the anticipatory character of the a priori concepts of the understanding deserves our attention. According to Kant, they refer to the "form" of every possible experience, such that form is related to content as the anticipation is to what is anticipated. This is the basis for Kant's specific problem concerning the anticipations of perception. The problem lies in the fact that these anticipations, to the extent that they are related to the intensity of the sensations, anticipate not only

---

8. Ibid., A 166.
9. Ibid., A 166-67.

the form but also the matter of perceptions.[10] But even this anticipation occurs only in a formal, general sense.

It thus seems that the structure of anticipation that characterizes the concept is closely tied to its formal nature. We must therefore consider the question whether the concrete concept (as defined by Hegel) is able to leave behind not only the level of the merely formal, but also the anticipatory character that is bound up with the formal. Hegel specified that the concept should exhibit an "adequacy" or correspondence of form and content. But it might seem that a concept of this sort, one that transcends [Aufhebung] the difference from content, must also rise above the structure of mere anticipation.

To decide this matter, we must consider the question whether Hegel was himself able to meet his own demand for the adequacy of form and content. In fact, every valid criticism of the content of Hegel's presentation (in his real-philosophical [realphilosophischen—as opposed to the "ideal philosophy" of the Logic] writings and lectures) in the philosophy of right, the philosophies of history and religion, and even the philosophy of nature, tells against the claim that he actually met the demand for an adequacy of form and content. Even the difficult question concerning the relationship between logic and "real philosophy" [Realphilosophie] in the context of the Hegelian system has a place here: if the structures utilized in the real-philosophical parts of the system move beyond the circle of conceptual determinations offered within the logic, then the adequacy of form and content is no longer assured. In this case, the determinations in the logic must be demoted to merely formal representations. But to view them as such would be strictly opposed to Hegel's own understanding of his logic. For he explicitly protested against such a demotion, and could do so because he viewed the conceptual determinations within the logic as categories of the Absolute. Yet, precisely as such, they could be no more than anticipations.

---

10. Ibid., B 209.

Otherwise, the full richness of the actual world in all its details would have to proceed out of the Absolute Idea.

Reflection on the mutual adequacy of form and content determines the dialectical progress of thought in Hegel's *Logic*, as it does also (though in a different sense) in the *Phenomenology of Spirit*. In the latter case, such reflection concerns the correspondence of consciousness to itself, a correspondence that is claimed on every level but falsified by reflection on the content of consciousness. Thus one can say that the conceptual determinations in the *Logic*, and the various forms of consciousness (especially of self-consciousness) in the *Phenomenology of Spirit*, reveal themselves within the process of reflection to be mere anticipations of what is actually meant—right up to the culmination of both works: absolute knowledge in the *Phenomenology*, and Absolute Idea in the *Logic*. Yet even in the transition to self-consciousness in the *Phenomenology*, and correspondingly in the transition to the subjective logic of the Concept, we encounter leaps in which a certain violence is recognizable, due presumably to the striving for a systematic conclusion. A critical reconstruction of Hegel's presentation could work out the anticipatory character of self-consciousness in the *Phenomenology* and of the Concept in his *Logic*, in opposition to his own presentation. The result would be a relativizing of the conclusion of both works.

The critical interpretation of Kant and Hegel that I am suggesting makes contact with some of the views of transcendental Thomism in contemporary philosophy. According to Karl Rahner, an unthematized fore-conception [*Vorgriff*] of being in its unlimited extension is the condition for grasping any finite essences at all. In making his case, Rahner appeals to some points of departure in Thomas Aquinas.[11] He might

---

11. Thomas Aquinas, *Summa theologica*, I, q. 84 a.7 ad 3: *excessus*. Regarding Rahner's use of the word "anticipation" [*Vorgriff*], see Kugelmann, *Antizipation*, pp. 207-35, especially the critical remarks on pp. 226ff.

also have appealed to the famous passage from Descartes's *Meditations*, particularly to its implicit coaffirmation of absolute being.[12] In this assumption [of absolute being] I agree with Rahner, as I do also regarding the impossibility of capturing this unthematized intuition through reflection. Nevertheless, I am not sure that one should characterize this phenomenon with Rahner as a fore-conception, that is, as anticipation. For there is no particular knowledge or representation of a thing that would be able to conceive in advance the experience of that thing. The infinite horizon, which unthematically precedes all experience of finite entities and concepts, has more the form of an intuitive seeing or a feeling. Concepts formed within this horizon have an anticipatory character, as do also assertions, which (as J. B. Lotz has correctly written) look forward to truth itself and thus also to being. Yet it is precisely the anticipatory function of the categories and concepts which Rahner has neglected.[13]

The concept of anticipation expresses in an integrated way the two-sidedness which arises in both the concept and the judgment in their relationship to things. On the one hand, both concepts and judgments claim for themselves an identity with the thing conceived: the thing whose concept is offered, or the state of affairs expressed through the assertorical or categorical judgment. On the other hand, the concept, as the "mere" concept of the thing that we attempt to conceptualize, is different from it, just as the judgment, as a "mere" assertion," is different from the asserted state of affairs. The

---

12. Descartes, *Meditations* III, §§ 23-24; see above, chap. 2 n. 5.

13. The use of the term "transcendental" for the arguments of transcendental Thomism can be misleading because these arguments (correctly) go beyond the Kantian search for the conditions of knowledge that are built into the subject prior to all experience. If, in Descartes's sense, the Infinite is the condition for the experience of the finite of any sort, even that of the subject itself, then the separation between the subject and the thing-in-itself, and thus the position of transcendental subjectivism, has thereby already been abandoned.

concept of anticipation, then, is able to unite both aspects—the identity with the thing and the difference from it. In the process the relationship between identity and difference is determined temporally: the anticipation is not yet identical in every respect with the anticipated thing; it remains exposed to the risk of untruth, of a failure to grasp. Yet, given the presupposition that the thing will appear in its full form sometime in the future, in the anticipation the thing is already present.

The demand for an adequacy of form and content is associated with that aspect of the concept according to which it is the concept of the thing itself and hence identical with that thing. If anticipation is to comprehend the two elements of identity and difference within the essence of the concept, then the question of the adequacy (or correspondence) of form and content is raised also with respect to it. The form of anticipation must correspond to the peculiar character of whatever it is that we claim is grasped anticipatorily and—at least given the limitations of finitude—can only be grasped in that way.

Could it be that the anticipatory form of knowledge corresponds to an element of the "not yet" within the very reality toward which knowing is directed? This must be the case if, given the limitations of finite knowledge, anticipation is to be more than a preliminary stage that one could leave behind by grasping the concept of the thing. Not only our knowing but also the identity of things themselves are not yet completely present in the process of time. From Dilthey's analysis of the historicity of experiencing, we learn that even the meaning of the events and things that we experience changes with the alteration of the context over the course of time. At first, this is a matter only of their meaning for us; the meaning that belongs to the events and things in and of themselves is something quite different. The latter meaning would be identical with the particular essence of the events and things, that is, with the meaning that belongs to them in themselves. The essence of things and events is not to be equated automatically with their meaning for us.

But can these two elements really be separated from each other? Is the essence that pertains to the things and events themselves a matter of indifference for the meaning that they have for me? In the first place, it is clear that events and things themselves already stand within contexts that change over the course of time. Only Dilthey's notion of life—which he narrowed down to the human life in contrast to the natural world—hindered him from applying his category of meaning, and the standpoint of the historicity of meaning, to the question of the essence of natural events and things. Had he done so, he would have seen that even the essence of events and forms within the natural world changes over the course of time; that is, what they are changes, their *ti ēn einai*. Only at the end of their movement through time, or even at the end of more complex series of events, could anyone decide what actually makes up their distinctive character, their essence. At that time, however, one would have to maintain that this had been the essence of the thing in question from the very beginning. The decision concerning the being that stands at the end of the process has retroactive power. A zinnia is already a zinnia as a cutting and remains one during the entire process of its growth up to blossoming, even though the flower bears its name on account of its blossom. If there were only a single such flower, we could not determine its nature in advance; and yet over the period of its growth it would still be what it revealed itself to be at the end. It would possess its essence through anticipation, though only at the end of the developmental process would one be able to know that this was its essence.

The Aristotelian doctrine of natural movement already sought to do justice to this state of affairs. Aristotle viewed the reality of beings—their actuality *(energeia)*, whose content is the idea or concept *(eidos)*—as the goal *(telos)* of their becoming. The result of becoming is an entelechy or completeness [*entelecheia:* actuality, fulfillment, completedness]: literally, having the *telos* within. As motion, *energeia* is directed toward the *entelecheia*.[14]

Note that Aristotle sometimes uses the term "completeness" *(entelecheia)* as a label for the motion that leads toward the goal: "motion is the not yet completed entelechy of what is moved."[15] If motion is understood as a goal-directed becoming, then the goal at which it aims, which will be "completely" reached at the end, must somehow be already present and efficacious during the motion; otherwise, what is moving could not move itself toward the goal. Entelechy therefore means both being at the goal and the way in which the goal is present and efficacious in the movement that leads to it—namely, as something which is absent and not yet attained. When one considers that the *telos* is at the same time the reality of the thing, its idea *(eidos)*, then one must grant that this *entelecheia* which is already present in the process of becoming is a form of presence of the thing's essence, although the thing will be completely there only at the end of its becoming.

If one allows this description (strange as it may seem) to sink in a bit, holding back the overused metaphor of seedlike predisposition and development, it becomes clear that the presence of the *entelecheia* in the process of becoming has an anticipatory structure; it implies an anticipatory reality of the *eidos* before its full realization. Had Aristotle based his description of motion solely on individual motions, he would have to have spoken of a *retroactive* causality of the *telos* during the course of becoming; the becoming would have to be the becoming of a being of a particular sort, as becomes clear at the end of the process. But precisely at this point Aristotle expanded his inquiry beyond the analysis of

---

14. Aristotle *Metaphysics* 1047a 30ff., 1050a 21ff.

15. Aristotle *Physics* 257b 8: "and motion is an incomplete fulfillment of the movable" *(estin d' hē kinēsis entelecheia kinētou atelēs).*

individual motions: he argued that what in one respect is becoming is in another respect already present: what is later (in the individual case) from the standpoint of origination is earlier from the standpoint of the species and essence.[16] As a result, the origination of what is completely new remains outside the purview of the Aristotelian doctrine of motion—even though, in his analysis of individual motion, Aristotle came very close to a deeper insight.

It was only with Dilthey's analysis of the historicity of experience that the breakthrough came: the retroactive constitution of the essence of a thing that is becoming from its end. In Aristotle's treatment, the possibility of extending his analysis of motion in this manner remains obscured because of his conviction that essential forms are timeless and immutable.[17] Nevertheless, we could take his analysis of individual motion—independent of all physical research into motion, which is simply not concerned with how the [essence or] "what it is to be" of things is constituted—as the starting point for a new definition of the concept of substance, one that would consider the viewpoint of time and becoming as the medium that constitutes the whatness of things. Things would then be what they are, substances, retroactively from the outcome of their becoming on the one hand, and on the other in the sense of anticipating the completion of their process of becoming, their history.

Such a conception is able to give an adequate account of the individuality even of natural entities. Of course, in view of the needs of everyday interaction, the redefinition might appear overly artificial in most cases, since ordinarily the orientation toward typical and self-repeating forms—the sort of forms to which the Aristotelian doctrine of motion is suited—represents a sufficient approximation. Nonetheless, a new definition of the concept of substance (of the sort I have

---

16. Aristotle *Metaphysics* 1049b-1050.
17. Ibid., 1033b 5ff., 16ff.

suggested here) is able to do justice both to the fundamental reservations that have been raised against the concept in its classical form and to the demand that time be incorporated into our understanding of being. Furthermore, it is able to avoid the weaknesses of atomistic approaches—according to which enduring forms are constituted out of elementary events—such as the one developed by Whitehead.

Any renewal of the concept of substance gives rise to the task of clarifying the relations between this sort of philosophical description and the natural-scientific descriptions of material processes. I have not taken on that task here. The distinction between these two modes of description is considerable: the natural-scientific description is primarily interested in laying hold of lawlike relations within natural processes, while philosophy seeks to clarify the question concerning the constitution of the essential forms of being. Any attempt to explore the relations between the philosophical question and the scientific description of natural processes would have to turn its attention not only to the atomistic mode of description within science but also to the role of the field concept [within physics]. This latter concept helps us to understand the overwhelming extent to which repetition within elementary processes serves as the basis for the formation of more complex forms; it is also able to clarify the formation of such forms themselves. The appeal to the field concept is not surprising when one recalls that, at its origin, it was just as philosophical a concept as that of Logos: the oldest field concepts were developed within the teachings of ancient philosophers concerning spirit *(pneuma).*[18]

---

18. According to M. Jammer, the teaching of Anaximenes on *pneuma* as *archē* was already "a field concept in principle." Jammer views the Stoics' teaching on *pneuma* as the "direct forerunner of the field concept." See his article "Feld, Feldtheorie," in *Historisches Worter-buch der Philosophie,* ed. Joachim Ritter (Basel: Schwabe, 1972), 2:923-26 (quote from p. 923).

In conclusion, I would like to note once again the relation of the above comments to the perspective of Christian eschatology. The connection between being and time makes it possible to forge a much closer connection between philosophical reflection and the biblical experience of reality. This same connection can be achieved through an understanding of being as the anticipation of the truth concerning its essence, a truth that is revealed only at the end of its course of development. In view of the fact that all events and forms are intertwined within the context of the world as a whole, this course of development cannot merely culminate with the end of an individual life. This is one of the reasons that Heidegger's interpretation of Dasein's wholeness, namely, as the anticipation of its end in death, remains overly one-sided, in that he isolates the individual question of existence from its social context. For this reason, Heidegger's work remains inferior to the analysis of the historicity of existence in Dilthey (by whom he was otherwise inspired). Like the historicists, Dilthey sought the final decision concerning the meaning of the individual's life—and the meaning of the other details that are linked to them—in the broader context of history. From Jewish apocalyptic we can trace the notion that the end of worldly history will bring fully to light all of its events and the life of each individual human being. But the end of history is not nothingness. The end of time (as we saw in Plotinus) is eternity. It is from the standpoint of this end that the essence of each individual thing, the manner in which it has anticipated eternity, will be decided.

PART TWO

METAPHYSICS AND THEOLOGY

CHAPTER 6

ATOMISM, DURATION, FORM: DIFFICULTIES WITH PROCESS PHILOSOPHY

WHOEVER COMES in contact with process philosophy today encounters it more often than not in the form of Whitehead's philosophy. This was the way it was for me when I was guest professor in 1963 at the University of Chicago and ran into an entire school of Whitehead adherents in the theological faculty (not, I must say, in the philosophical faculty). Consequently, for the sake of my own intellectual survival, I had to come to grips quickly and intensively with the writings of this philosopher, who was at that time hardly known on the continent of Europe.

I found the experience enriching; it made up for a certain lack in the great tradition of German Idealism. One feels in Idealism the need for a philosophy of nature adequate to the demands of our century, for a metaphysics that, from the outset, integrates the awareness of the world as mediated by contemporary knowledge of nature with human experience as disclosed by the humanities and social sciences. The more time I spent with Whitehead, however, the more I was shocked by the rather dogmatic way in which he is read in the United States within the school of process theology, a school which has in the meantime become quite influential. In that school Whitehead is taken to be an entirely self-sufficient systematic thinker and, as such, authoritative, like Aristotle in the High Scholasticism of the thirteenth century. He is not read as an exponent of a broader current of process thought, in the context of which his philosophical approach represents only one of the options which can be (and in part already have been) pursued.

If one considers Whitehead's philosophy in its relationship to thinkers such as Henri Bergson and Samuel Alexander (to name only two), then one becomes aware of different versions of the process-philosophical perspective. It becomes clear that a process-philosophical approach—one which dismisses the notion of a timelessly identical substance—is not necessarily tied to the specific assumptions that Whitehead made: his doctrine that discrete emergent "occasions" or elementary events[1] are the ultimate realities, and his view of "eternal objects" as potentials for the self-realization of these occasions.

Let us turn to the first assumption, namely, that event-like "occasions" or "actual entities" form the final real things which constitute the world.[2] This thesis implies an atomistic ontology. Whitehead himself says, "Thus the ultimate metaphysical truth is atomism," and he calls his philosophy "an atomic theory of actuality."[3] He takes the continuum of reality to be a phenomenon that is derived from the discretely emergent actual entities. Taken by itself, the continuum is only possibility, a "potentiality for division";[4] it is divided by the actual entities. With this claim, Whitehead enters into conflict not only with Newton's theory of absolute space and absolute time but also with Bergson. In Bergson's type of

---

1. More precisely, "actual occasion" designates the primary constituents of events: "an actual occasion is the limiting type of an event with only one member" (*PR* [chap. 4 n. 7 above], p. 73 [113]).

2. Ibid., p. 18 (27).

3. Ibid., pp. 35 (53), 27 (40), respectively.

4. Ibid., p. 67 (104).

process philosophy, "duration," and with it a form of continuum, is fundamental. Bergson's "duration" is the continuum of becoming itself, while for Whitehead becoming is
not continuous; in line with the paradoxes of Zeno, he asserts,
"there can be no continuity of becoming."[5]

On this question, Samuel Alexander sides with Bergson—although Alexander, anticipating Whitehead's somewhat later remarks,[6] criticizes Bergson for setting up an
opposition between space and time. The "spatialization" of
time—which Bergson had judged to be the work of the
understanding, and which he blamed in large part for the
errors of traditional substance metaphysics—Alexander
takes to be the essence of time itself.[7] Only space can make
continuity possible, not only because a moment of time can
be common to different places, but above all because, in-
versely, many consecutive events can occur at the same
place.[8] A succession of instants by themselves would lack
continuity: "it would consist of perishing instants."[9] Continuity, which Whitehead later secured by his subtle theory
of "eternal objects" and their ingression into the world of
actual occasions, is guaranteed in Alexander's thought by a
space which has not yet been relativized. To this extent we
can understand Alexander as Whitehead's precursor.

However, Alexander's conception of the infinity of
space-time, as the condition for the determination of finitude,
is opposed to Whitehead's. Following Samuel Clarke and
also Kant's Transcendental Aesthetic, Alexander thinks of
finitude and, above all, individual instants or points of time

---

5. Ibid., p. 35 (53).
6. Ibid., p. 321 (489-90).
7. Samuel Alexander, *Space, Time and Deity* (New York: Macmillan, [1920], 1966), 1:143; cf. p. 149 (henceforth *STD*).
8. Ibid., 1:48-49.
9. Ibid., 1:45.

as limitations of infinity. "The infinite is not what is not finite, but the finite is what is not infinite."[10]

Like Levinas today, Alexander refers back to Descartes when he defines the constitutive meaning of the infinite as making it possible to conceive of the finite as such. This means, of course, that atomism cannot be advocated as the final metaphysical truth. Alexander shares Bergson's conception that movement is primordial, and hence that it is always holistic and continuous.[11] "Motion is not a succession of point-instants, but rather a point-instant is the limiting case of a motion."[12] Distinguishing between point-instants is the product of intellectual abstraction. "They are in fact . . . inseparable from the universe of motion; they are elements in a continuum."[13] Alexander consequently moves close to Spinoza: space-time is the whole of that which exists, the infinite, which precedes all finite actuality.[14]

With Bergson and Alexander on one side, and Whitehead's event-atomism on the other, we are faced with two fundamental and alternative approaches to process thinking. To be sure, Alexander attempted to distinguish infinite space-time both from the category of substance and from that of a whole that precedes its parts,[15] the latter because, in his view, such a whole is always to be thought of as composed of parts. However, with regard to motion at least, he did speak of the whole of motion as being prior to its individual space-time instants.[16] In contrast, Whitehead proceeds from the ontological priority of discrete events or their components. But does he not thereby fall into the logical aporias of every

10. Ibid., 1:42.
11. Ibid., 1:149.
12. Ibid., 1:321.
13. Ibid., 1:325.
14. Ibid., 1:339ff.
15. Ibid., 1:338ff.
16. Ibid., 1:321.

atomistic metaphysics? Plato stated the case long ago: without the One, the others can be neither one nor many; there would be absolutely nothing.[17] Many ones are many of the same (abstract One), but they are also many in relationship and so parts of a whole; if they do not form a totality, then they cannot be thought of as exemplifying the same One. In any case, an encompassing unity must be presupposed if atoms are to be conceivable as unities at all.

If I am not mistaken, Whitehead nowhere discusses the logical difficulties inherent in the systematic concept of atomism, although in *Adventures of Ideas* he does discuss various forms of atomism.[18] Whitehead distances himself from the sort of atomism—going back to Democritus, Epicurus, and Lucretius—from which the positivist interpretation of modern natural science is derived. Under such an interpretation, the atoms are only externally related, according to the principle of randomness; the relations are no less external in Newton's mechanics, where they express laws imposed from without by the will of God.[19] In contrast, Whitehead sees Plato as the originator of a way of looking at things which understands laws (and thus the relationships they regulate between things) as immanent in the things themselves.[20] Whitehead himself is inclined to this conception.

Even earlier, in *Science and the Modern World,* Whitehead attacks any description of relations between events that is given solely in external terms, which he finds in the usual accounts of space-time relations.[21] Instead, insofar as the individual events are constituted by the relationships in

---

17. Plato *Parmenides* 165ff.

18. A. N. Whitehead, *Adventure of Ideas* (New York: Macmillan Free Press, 1933), pp. 125ff. (henceforth *AI*).

19. Ibid., p. 127.

20. Ibid., pp. 121ff.

21. Whitehead, *Science and the Modern World,* 2nd ed. (New York: Macmillan Free Press, 1925), p. 115 (henceforth *SMW*).

which they stand, these are internal to the events: "the relationships of an event are internal, so far as . . . they are
constitutive of what the event is in itself."[22] According to
Whitehead, the acceptance of such inner relationships requires viewing the individual event as subjective—a subjectivity which integrates the manifold relations constituting the
event.[23] When this occurs, these internal relations represent
themselves as acts of the event itself and, as such, are called
"prehensions." In Whitehead's main work, *Process and Reality*, this concept stands at the center of his analyses, while the
discussion of external and internal relations fades into the
background (though even here "prehensions" are still defined as "concrete facts of relatedness").[24] Each individual
event prehends all the other events of the world that it knows.
The other events it encounters must be appropriated as its
own: "each actual entity includes the universe, by reason of
its determinate attitude towards every element in the universe."[25]

It may appear that the one-sidedness of atomism is
thereby counterbalanced. The thesis that every individual
event is conditioned by the totality of all the others does do
apparent justice to the constitutive meaning of the whole for

---

22. Ibid., p. 98.

23. Ibid., p. 115.

24. *PR*, p. 22 (32). The relations' fading into the background may
be connected with the fact that relations may now be characterized as
reciprocal ("the complex of mutual prehensions," *PR*, p. 194 [295]),
while *SMW* still distinguishes, in an Aristotelian sense, between internal and external relations (analogous to the difference between *relatio
realis* and *relatio rationis* in Scholastic philosophy). Cf. also *PR*, pp. 222-23
(340) and 50 (79).

25. *PR*, p. 45 (71-72). Cf. p. 80 (123): "each actual entity is a locus
for the universe," a view expressed earlier in *The Concept of Nature*
(Cambridge: Cambridge University Press, 1920), p. 152 (hereafter *CN*).
Later Whitehead relates this idea to the concept of a physical field (*PR*,
p. 80 [123-24]).

the individual. Still, one should observe that Whitehead does not speak directly of the universe having a meaning for the individual, but only hints at it indirectly, based on the relationship of every event to every other "element" of the universe. Only this latter sense is expressed when he writes: "every actual entity springs from *that* universe which there *is for it*."[26] Since the universe (or the space-time continuum) is not given as a real whole to the individual event, it is always the individual event itself which must integrate into a whole the manifold relationships into which it enters. Consequently, as many perspectives on the universe arise as there are events that emerge.

It is no accident that Leibniz comes to mind at this point. Whitehead explicitly refers to Leibniz's doctrine of monads: "I am using the same notion, only I am toning down his monads into the unified events in space and time."[27] With his thesis of the "windowlessness" of monads, however, Leibniz would have denied the concrete reality of internal relations. For Leibniz, the monads do not stand in real relationships to each other but only mirror the primary monad and the universe created by it, each refracting the universe from its own finite position. According to Leibniz, then, natural laws are as much externally imposed on the world (viz., by God) as they were in Descartes.[28] Whitehead, on the contrary, wants to understand the laws of nature as emerging out of the reciprocal relationships of the things themselves, as expressing these reciprocal relations. Hence individual events appear to him not only as reflections of the universe but also as the *subjects* of the creative integration of the manifold relations which constitute them. The spatiotemporal continuum is then taken to be the result of an abstraction from the

---

26. *PR*, p. 80 (124).
27. *SMW*, p. 68.
28. Cf. *AI*, p. 138.

concrete event itself, out of which the relationships among the "actual entities" emerge.[29]

In the end, Whitehead's theory of the prehensions does not really counterbalance the one-sidedness of atomism. For the whole of the universe (or of the spatiotemporal continuum), on Whitehead's account, has no inherent integrity of its own in the way that the monadlike events do. For Leibniz, the universe, established in the mind of God, precedes each individual creature and is only mirrored by the creature. In Whitehead's thought, however, God is not the creator but only the cocreator of all real events; consequently, the actual occasions, as self-constitutive, are themselves the ground of the continuum that expresses their "nexus"—the continuum is derived from them.

Whitehead appeals to the subjectivity of individual events as the central force that integrates the manifold of self-constituting relationships. Using this concept, he challenges the materialistic description of natural processes, which settles for merely external relationships, with a more profound vision.[30] But the idea of a self-constituting subjectivity of actual occasions leads to new difficulties. On the one hand, the actual occasion or actual entity ought to be the ultimate constituent of the physical universe. On the other hand, these ultimate constituents of the universe can be broken down further into the relations or "prehensions" which constitute them. Whitehead's response is that the analysis of an "actual entity" is feasible only in thought: "The actual entity is divisible; but it is in fact undivided."[31] If, however, the analysis of the actual occasion into the prehensions (or internal relations) which constitute it is feasible only through mental abstraction, then we are faced with a problem. How is it possible to continue to interpret the actual

---

29. Cf. *CN*, p. 78.
30. *SMW*, pp. 97-98.
31. *PR*, p. 227 (347).

occasion itself as a process with different phases, in which it generates itself, while also asserting that the end phase of this process is identical with the complete duration of the event?[32]

The entire presentation of a "genetic division" in *Process and Reality*, with its differentiation of various phases in the self-constitution of the event,[33] raises the suspicion that Whitehead has confused the abstract and the concrete, thereby committing the "fallacy of misplaced concreteness" which he has often astutely criticized in other thinkers. Whitehead holds that we cannot, in fact, divide the actual occasion further but can only abstractly differentiate the relationships that constitute its identity. If so, he cannot in the same breath characterize the actual occasion as being the result of a process in which these relations, distinguishable only in the abstract, are actually integrated. Even more confusingly, the relations themselves are said to be constituted only by the actual occasion.

Yet such a position is clearly necessary if Whitehead wants to be able to affirm the subjectivity of actual occasions as *causae sui*.[34] If one conceives of the actual occasion as determined merely by the collision of the intersecting relations that constitute it at a moment of time, then the actual occasion is thought only as an object. As such, it cannot be separated from its field; it is nothing more than a singularity of the field ("the systematically adjusted set of modifications of the field").[35] It would seem that the subjectivity of the event

---

32. Ibid., pp. 26 (39), 283 (434), respectively.

33. Cf., e.g., ibid., pp. 26-27 (40), 248-49 (380-81).

34. Ibid., pp. 86 (131), 88 (135); cf. pp. 25-26 (38).

35. *CN*, p. 190. In *CN*, Whitehead still did not view the "point-flash" or "event-particle" as the ultimate real component of the natural world: "You must not think of the world as ultimately built up of event particles," he expressly says there (p. 172; cf. p. 59). The world is rather "a continuous stream of occurrences which we can discriminate into finite events forming by their overlappings and containings of each other and separations a spatio-temporal structure" (pp. 172-73; cf. also *AI*, p. 161).

must be assumed if the event's independence is to be at all conceivable. Thus, such subjectivity is a necessary condition of Whitehead's atomistic interpretation of reality. Now if the independence of actual occasions is thought of as self-constitution, then it would seem to follow that the actual occasion itself must be reconceived as a process which integrates that which precedes it and thereby constitutes its own identity. This conception is self-contradictory, however, for the actual occasions are claimed to be the ultimate components of reality and not themselves integrations of more primitive components. This fundamental thesis cannot be reconciled with the assumption of the actual occasions' self-constitution.

Whitehead's "genetic analysis" of the actual occasion clearly amounts to an extrapolation which forces the experiential structures of more highly organized forms of life onto the interpretation of actual occasions. Whitehead himself described this procedure of his speculative philosophy as the method of imaginative generalization; and it is precisely the principle of self-constitution as "creativity" which forms, in his own philosophy, the central application of this method.[36]

Whitehead's doctrine of the subjectivity of actual occasions shares many individual features with the philosophical psychology of William James. More specifically, such features include, on the one hand, the momentary character of the ego and, on the other, the description of each ego-instant as being a momentary integration of experience, and especially an integration of the past of such ego-instants. Presumably, Whitehead's theory of the subjectivity of actual occasions can be interpreted, to a very large extent, as a generalization of the idea of the ego in William James's psychology, a generalization achieved by applying this idea to the interpretation of the foundations of physics. It was not for nothing that Whitehead placed James, alongside Bergson and Dewey,

---

36. *PR*, pp. 5 (8), 7 (11); cf. pp. 4ff. (7ff.).

among the thinkers to whom his chief work [*Process and Reality*] is especially indebted. In *Science and the Modern World*, he even compared James to Descartes as a founder of a new era of philosophy.[37]

The demonstration of connections such as these is certainly not enough to substantiate any objection to Whitehead's claims. The procedure of imaginative generalization obviously plays a considerable role in any formation of philosophical concepts. Whitehead himself says, however, that such a procedure has the character of "tentative formulations" and that it requires, along with inner consistency and coherence, confrontation with facts: "Speculative boldness must be balanced by complete humility before logic, and before fact."[38]

Measured by this yardstick, the use of the structures of subjectivity for interpreting actual occasions seems illegitimate. James's psychology of subjectivity has to do with a real succession of moments of experience, while Whitehead's thought cannot claim any such real succession in the genesis of the individual actual occasion. James's psychology of the ego can conceive each individual moment of experience as a new integration of previous experience because the successive moments are really distinct and because the relation of the later to the earlier (as the integration of human experiential moments) constitutes the special quality of human, subjective behavior in the medium of experience, reflection, and memory. For his part, Whitehead can appeal only to the factual universal relatedness of all events as the basis for applying the Jamesian model of subjectivity to the relationship that obtains between newly emergent events and all other events (including their predecessors).

It is doubtful that the similarities here have sufficient reach. According to James, the ego, which always emerges

---

37. *SMW*, pp. 129-30.
38. *PR*, pp. 8 (12), 17 (25) respectively.

momentarily, in no way relates itself to all preceding events but only to those earlier experiences made present to it by memory. The human faculty of memory, however, is a highly specialized function which cannot, without further ado, be attributed to all natural processes. Moreover, the integration performed by the momentarily emerging ego is, in James, conditioned by the fact that the human body, on the one hand, and the "social self" (composed of the expectations of a social identity that face the individual), on the other, do not emerge in a pointlike manner. Instead, they represent continua, in relation to which the point-by-point synthesis of the ego can function as the principle of novelty and creativity.

Whitehead's speculative extrapolation of the principle of subjective integration that emerges moment by moment may overestimate the measure of uniformity encountered in the real world. The generalization of the structure of the human ego, as understood by James (but not tied to the problematic of the self as distinguished from the ego), paradoxically reduces the special status of the higher forms of natural evolution, especially the evolution of life, to the level of elementary processes. These more complex forms of natural evolution Whitehead merely describes as diversely ordered series, or "societies" of actual occasions. Because certain abstract structural elements are reproduced in each individual succession and systematically modified, the societies appear as stable unities without finally being such. In *Process and Reality*, the relatively brief treatment of this topic suggests that the ontological dignity of stable forms is considered secondary to the structure of actual occasions. Were we to suppose, however, that the correct description of actual occasions would, in principle, decipher the code for the formation of all higher forms (since such occasions are the basis for all higher forms), then we would fall into the mode of thinking of materialism, which is precisely what Whitehead wished to challenge.

The fact that the emergence of broader forms cannot be

derived from the actual occasions which supposedly compose them shows once again that the unity of the field cannot be reduced to the elementary pointlike events that appear in it. With respect to the metaphysical relevance of form as actuality, not merely as structure in the sense of Whitehead's "eternal objects," we also see how one-sided the atomistic interpretation of reality is: it cannot treat wholeness and individual discreteness as metaphysical principles of equal importance.

Remarkably, however, it is precisely Whitehead's genetic analysis of actual occasions with its paradoxes that offers constructive new perspectives upon which to build. According to Whitehead, the phases of formation are not to be thought of as *temporally* successive, since the actual occasion is what it is as an undivided unity. Therefore, representing the occasion as a process of formation appears paradoxical to us. But Whitehead's analyses do illuminate our understanding of processes whose phases certainly must be thought of as temporally successive, yet in which the goal of becoming [*das Werdeziel*] for the form has always been present. All life processes, for example, seem to be of this nature. In the process of its formation, the plant or animal is always this plant or this animal, although its specific nature comes fully to light only in the result of its formation. By way of anticipation, it is always that which it will become only in the process of its formation. The identity of its being is assuredly not that of a momentary occasion, but resides in the identity of its nature, of its essential form, which endures over the course of time. By anticipating its essential form in the process of its own formation, a being's substantial identity is linked together with the notion of process.

In Whitehead's genetic analysis of elementary processes, the concepts of "subjective aim" and "superject" play a similar role. Already in *Process and Reality*, Whitehead speaks occasionally of anticipatory feelings using the notion of subjective aim; he then expands greatly on this in *Adven-*

tures of Ideas.[39] Even in the latter book he does not go so far as to describe the significance of anticipation for the formation of the subject, in the sense that its subjectivity is constituted out of its future, a future that already determines the present by way of anticipation. Rather, for Whitehead anticipation means that the subject, constituting itself in the present, includes also its future relevance for others (its "objective immortality") in the act of its self-constitution.

Whitehead did not thereby exhaust the theoretical potential of the notion of anticipation that is implied in the concept of "subjective aim." Aristotle's analysis of motion, which forms the background to all teleological descriptions of process, made fuller use of this notion. In the case of natural motions, Aristotle interpreted the anticipation of the final state within the moved object itself as entelechy.[40] By doing so, he reinterpreted the effect of the future goal upon the present becoming along the lines of the influence that a living organism's seed has on its future goal. Aristotle nevertheless spoke of an effect of the end upon the process of becoming. Whitehead never speaks in this way because he sees becoming in each of its stages as self-constitutive. This is why, despite his use of teleological language, the element of anticipation cannot really become constitutive in his interpretation of subjectivity.

The idea of the radical self-creation of each actual occasion is the reason why Whitehead's metaphysics cannot be reconciled with the biblical idea of creation or (therefore) with the biblical idea of God. To be sure, American process theology has attempted to interpret Whitehead's concept of creativity in terms of a divine creative activity.[41] But in White-

---

39. Cf. *PR*, pp. 278 (424-25), 214-15 (327-28); *AI*, pp. 194-95.

40. See pp. 105-6 above.

41. So, especially, John Cobb, *God and the World* (Philadelphia: Westminster, 1965), pp. 42-66. God, who encounters humans as their future by calling them to new possibilities, is, according to Cobb, a force

head's thought itself, the constitution of each actual entity's subjectivity remains always a self-constitution, and this despite the dependence of each actual entity upon God, who provides it with the conditions of its self-realization through its "initial aim." This stems from the fact that Whitehead ties the teleological structure of formation to actual occasions. He

---

(p. 59), indeed a liberating force (p. 64), but also at the same time the ground of our being and of the order of nature (p. 65). Can such statements about a creative work of God justifiably fit into the conceptual scheme of Whitehead's philosophy? Don't they rather demand a reworking of the fundamental categories of his system? According to the remarks on "God and the World" in *PR* (pp. 342-51 [519-33]), God is not creator of the world (p. 346 [526]); or, in any case, he is just as much its creature as its creator (p. 348 [528]). How this conception differs from the Christian view of creation has been accurately portrayed by Langdon Gilkey in *Reaping the Whirlwind: A Christian Interpretation of History* (New York: Harper & Row, 1977), pp. 248ff. He asserts correctly that Whitehead's thought on philosophy "must be reinterpreted and in part refashioned" (p. 114). But has Gilkey taken sufficient account of the thoroughly radical changes demanded by such a view? He finds Whitehead's concept of "creativity" obscure and even incoherent (p. 250) because in *PR*, p. 21 (31-32), it is characterized as the principle which brings forth new entities, while on p. 18 (27) only events, as actual entities themselves, form the ultimately real elements which compose the world (Gilkey, *Reaping*, p. 414 n. 34). Perhaps this difficulty is resolved by viewing the principle of creativity as expressing nothing more than the self-constitution of the events in their "subjectivity." Still, Gilkey feels that the incoherence in Whitehead's conception cannot be overcome "unless it is reinterpreted as the divine power of being, as the activity of God as creator preserver" (p. 414 n. 34). The question then is whether Gilkey, along with Whitehead, can still talk of the self-creativity or "self-actualization" of the world or events, without sounding incoherent himself. A much deeper incursion into Whitehead's conceptual scheme seems necessary if enough room is to be cleared for the idea of a creator God. The idea of the self-constitutive subjectivity of the event itself would need to be altered, and since this idea is closely related to Whitehead's event atomism, both would have to be revised together. Of course, such a correction cannot be based upon some theological postulate. Its necessity can only be shown through philosophical argument.

claims for them the character of processes but does not allow for temporal extension in the sense of a succession of phases in time: actual occasions, which supposedly compose all else, are considered momentary and undivided.

The matter would be otherwise if we limited White-head's genetic analysis to processes that take place in time, instead of using it to explain the constitution of actual occasions. Then the "subjective aim" of the process would have to do with the actual, still-to-come future of each one's own essential completion. This future completion would not depend on present decisions alone, though it would eventually be reached or not reached by such decisions. Correspondingly, the anticipation of one's own essential completion in the future would gain greater significance for the constitution of subjectivity; the latter could no longer be identified with the self-creation of present decisions, but would be dependent on the whole of one's own essential completion being manifested in each present.

Such a conception would certainly no longer be that of an atomistic metaphysic. It would no longer attribute subjectivity to the randomness of actual occasions. Rather, from the impossibility of such attribution (because it involves the paradoxical assumption of a nontemporal process), we can construct an argument for the claim that the independence of finite being and subjectivity can increase along with the complexity of forms rather than be fully expressed at the outset in the elementary occasions. The unity of the field, from which actual occasions proceed, would no longer be traceable back to a network of relations that is itself first constituted by these occasions. Rather, we would have to conceive the unity of the field together with the unity (also underivable from but composed of actual occasions) of the forms that appear in increasing differentiation on higher levels of natural process.

Again, such a view of the matter would no longer be atomistic, because it does not limit reality (in the sense of what is actual) to the undivided actual occasions. This is hardly reason enough, however, to remove such a view from the circle of process philosophies, even though it holds to the idea of an essential identity of that which continues to become throughout the process of its formation. The unity encompasses the whole process and so links the fundamental intention of the concept of substance with the process perspective. It is precisely in this direction that Whitehead's analysis of genetic processes, with his concept of the subject as the "superject" of its own process of formation, has provided important new impulses, even if these impulses bear fruit only after they have been liberated from the confinement of momentary actual occasions and the atomism which accompanies them in Whitehead's thought. In rethinking the matter in this way, we also free process thought from the aporias which have arisen within a theoretical context burdened by these assumptions.

CHAPTER 7

THEOLOGY AND
THE CATEGORIES
"PART" AND "WHOLE"

WHEN THE CONCEPTS "part" and "whole" are designated as categories (or as one category in the relational expression "part and whole") and one wishes to raise the question of the significance of this category for a given science [*Wissenschaft*] as distinct from other sciences, it would seem appropriate to begin with a few comments concerning the key word "category" and the general relationship between categories and sciences. Of course, it will not be possible to develop and discuss this theme completely here, since the notion of category has played a central role in philosophical thought since Aristotle and been construed in quite diverse ways in various systematic philosophical schemes. Accordingly, its link to "science" (a term with its own multitude of meanings) has been the subject of widely differing proposals. Under these circumstances I can only sketch briefly the sense of the term "category" operational in the following sections. In this context I cannot provide justification for all the decisions made regarding the individual philosophical problems involved.

"Category" means literally a form of stating or asserting, that is, a *katēgorein*. This meaning has to do with a form of speech, and in particular with semantics rather than syntax. More precisely, it constitutes an element of meaning alongside others within the semantic structure of the act of asserting. Yet in the case of a category in the philosophical sense of the word we are not concerned with a concrete, individual unit of meaning—say, with a "statement-point," corresponding perhaps to the "accusation-point" which the word originally indicated—but rather with a general structural moment of the act of stating itself. The Aristotelian doctrine of the categories had already been developed in this direction, although the semantic meaning structure of the act of stating had not yet won its full independence from the syntactic structure of language. For this reason Aristotle aligned his doctrine of the categories so closely with the functions of sentences, with their diversity and reciprocal interrelationships.

Yet Aristotle did not develop his doctrine of the categories only as a doctrine of the meaning structures of language or of the assertion as a linguistic form, but also as a doctrine of the most general forms of what is [*des Seienden*]. This connection follows as a consequence of the semantic nature of the categories themselves, since they involve us with general, formal moments of stating or asserting: assertions are made *about something*. The elements of meaning found in language, or at least in linguistic assertions, are thus simultaneously structural forms of that which exists. To be sure, this is the case only under the additional condition that the assertions—as they themselves qua assertions always claim—are true. If we leave out of consideration the semantic forms of untrue assertions, we may conclude that categories are the general elements of meaning that are attributed both to true assertions and to the states of affairs which they grasp. In other words, categories are the general structural elements of *knowledge*, and that not merely of the general *form* of knowledge, as would be the case according to Kant's doctrine of the categories. Rather, they are the general structural elements of knowledge as knowledge of facts, and indeed of this knowledge in its totality.

131

That every category is related to the totality of knowledge (and thus also to the totality of what is) is already connoted by the level of generality Aristotle claimed for them. Such generality is nothing else than a formal, abstract aspect (and thus only one aspect among others) of this totality. The categories' relation to the totality of reality as comprehended by knowledge obtains even in the light of the fact that we never attain complete knowledge of this totality because of the finitude of human existence and human experience. But formulating categories in their generality is predicated on the possibility of doing so. Consequently, the totality of knowledge (and of what is) can only be *anticipated* in our consciousness, insofar as we all employ categories—whether unreflectively or with reflective awareness—and thereby show that they are not merely the inventions of philosophers.

The formation of categories can anticipate the totality of knowledge in two ways: either implicitly within the concrete individual cognition, in that its truth rests on the condition that it agrees with all other truths; or explicitly, in that this necessary relation to the totality of all truth itself becomes a theme for reflection. In the latter case, though, the totality of knowledge—and therefore also of reality—is comprehended merely as an abstract generality, and thus not as a concrete unity but as a plurality of abstract aspects. This is precisely the function of the categories: they are abstract, general aspects of knowledge (and thus also of what exists) in its totality. They depend upon the thematized anticipation of this totality, and from it stems their generality.

It has already become clear from this discussion that categories in the philosophical sense of the word (i.e., categories that make the claim to a strict generality not only of form but also of validity) cannot be derived directly from language about objects as it is articulated in assertions. Rather, they become accessible to analysis only through a reflection on their connections, implicit in individual assertions, with all other assertions and asserted states of affairs. But what claim can such reflection make to necessity? Isn't it possible to avoid reflecting in this way on the totality that underlies the formation of categorical notions? It would be avoidable only if we neglect the distinction between true and false assertions in considering the meaning structures of discourse that uses assertions, that is, if we limit ourselves merely to an examination of the linguistic form of such discourse. However, such a limitation only becomes possible when we abstract from the actual meaning structure of the assertion itself, since the assertion as linguistic form intends a state of affairs and claims correspondence with that state of affairs, that is, truth.

For this reason, the meaning structures of the words in a sentence cannot be reduced to their function within the context of the sentence and within the wider context of discourse. As the individual word has a reference (albeit incomplete) to an object, so also the sentence as judgment (assertion) has an objective reference. In this phenomenon the objective reference of the individual word within the sentence becomes determinate through the reciprocal explication of subject and predicate, and not merely through the subsumption of the subject under the idea contained in the predicate. The truth claim of an assertion is linked with this determinateness of the words in the sentence. Yet the realm of meaning relevant to the assertion extends not only to the implications of the words, themselves indeterminate, within the context of discourse, but also to the other states of affairs with which the asserted state of affairs stands in relationship. Therefore, one always says more than one wants to say. This applies both to what the sentence actually expresses within the context of a discourse, action, or social situation, and to the sphere of real givens within which the asserted state of affairs itself stands and the other states of affairs may be known—even when the speakers themselves are not aware of them.

The claim of every assertion (as knowledge of facts) to

truth means that we cannot avoid reflecting on the totality of all true assertions and thereby on the totality of what is—at least, as long as it is the case that an individual assertion can be true if and only if it coheres with all other true assertions. This is the foundation upon which, ultimately, both the coherence theory of truth and the legitimation of all systematic thought rest. This truth condition for the individual statement, however, can only become a theme of reflection for an anticipating consciousness. It can only be comprehended in the form of a plurality of aspects abstracted from the totality of knowledge and being, which as such (as a concrete totality) is not adequately accessible to or attainable for the finite consciousness. Thinkers have sought repeatedly to find ways to lay hold of the complete number of such aspects or categories. Yet if this were possible, we plainly should be able to reconstruct the totality of reality and experience, which is not in itself directly obtainable, out of the composition of its abstract aspects, at least as far as its general and thus essential structural elements are concerned.

However, this sort of systematics of categories has failed again and again. Even the assumption that there is only a finite number of such abstract general aspects of the totality of knowledge and being cannot be demonstrated. If one accepts C. F. von Weizsäcker's belief in an "inexhaustibility of the real through individual items of structural knowledge,"[1] then skepticism certainly seems appropriate regarding the question whether one should count on the number of the categories of what exists (and of knowledge) being finite. This does not exclude the possibility, however, that a finite number of aspects of experience may apply to the finitude of *human* existence. These aspects demand careful attention in our reflection upon the activity of true asserting, even though they may be in principle variable and surpassable.

---

1. C. F. von Weizsäcker, "Kontinuität und Möglichkeit," in *Zum Weltbild der Physik*, 6th ed. (1954), p. 227.

Consequently, just as a plurality of categories (understood as abstract aspects of the totality of what is) is related to the finitude of human existence as the locus of our experience and knowledge, so also is the fact that certain categories play a prominent role in our experience. Furthermore, it is due to the nature of our finitude that, within the various (and variously differentiated) realms of human experience, different categories may occupy the foreground as organizing principles of their respective subrealms. If, with Schleiermacher, one describes the areas of human experience by means of the concepts "science," "praxis," and "religion," one will end up with a different array of categories than if one distinguishes and coordinates these areas with Jürgen Habermas using the concepts "technical knowledge," "communication," and "reflection." Specific categories have a particular affinity to specific individual sciences and make possible their methodological approach to their given area of study, without detriment to the generality which each category expresses in its own way. This fact is based on the relation that we find between the division of experience into various areas and the categories that become central when we represent each of these areas. From the preceding discussion we can also understand what makes such categories so important in discussions of methodology. The categories allow us to relate individual states of affairs found in various areas of experience to the *totality* of reality, while preserving the way this totality is viewed within the guiding perspectives of the individual scientific disciplines. In this relation, the particularities of the different sciences and of their perspectives on reality correspond to the abstractness and particularity of the categories.

On the basis of these comments, it is now possible to raise the question of the role of specific categories for specific sciences. In this context, we can then also address the question of the significance of the category of the whole for theology.

Among the categories which form the basis for modern natural science and determine its field of objects, those of space and time must be mentioned prior to all others (see chap. 4 above). In saying this, I presuppose that space and time are not, or at least are not merely, forms of intuition in Kant's sense; rather, they are universal concepts. Intuition refers to objects in space and time and to their relationships to one another, but not to space and time as such; these, in their universality, have a categorical or unconditional character. The transformational equations for space and time in physics guarantee their homogeneity, which is the condition for all measurement and consequently also for all mathematico-quantitative description of natural processes. To these two categories classical physics added those of mass and force, as well as the category of law. All of these concepts are universally applicable elements of the description of nature as carried out within modern natural science, and thus authentic categories. Of these categories, that of law is the foundational category for the theoretical context of modern natural science, whose methodology it also significantly determines.

I would like to argue that the concept of the whole plays a fundamental role in the so-called human sciences [*Geisteswissenschaften*] similar to that of law in the natural sciences. Now this claim does not imply the well-known dualism of natural and human sciences. The concept of the whole, as a universal category, is also applicable to objects of nature, and it underlies the description of nature utilized in the natural sciences as well. For instance, the concept of the whole implicitly underlies the notion of a body or material point, as well as the more specific concepts of atom and molecule. In each of these instances, we have to do with a unit which can be regarded both as a whole composed of its parts and as a part or element itself. Furthermore, the category of the whole is an implicit component of the notion of systems as they are described in natural scientific formulas and represented in the system of these formulas.

Nevertheless, the category of the whole does not explicitly occupy the foreground in natural scientific description of natural processes. The ultimate reason for this may be that the totality of space and time is left undifferentiated [*vergleichgültigt*] because of the demands for homogeneity made by the transformational equations.[2] Dissimilarities in space and time become indifferent [*gleich-gültig*]: parts stand next to one another as having equal validity in principle and thus as exchangeable; they are no longer "parts" in the true sense, since they are no longer defined unmistakably by their position within the whole. It is this differentiation, and thus the individuality of the single occurrence, which natural science (and all nomological science) neglects. Such dimming of differences occurs, as we saw, through the homogeneity or homogenizing of space and time. The fact that similarly strict demands for homogeneity are not feasible within other areas of study indicates the limits to which mathematical methods can be applied to them on the model of the natural sciences.

While the concept of the whole is not fully absent from the natural sciences but is subordinated to their interest in nomological descriptions of natural processes, the so-called human sciences, by contrast, are primarily interested in individual appearances. Their concentration is on specific texts, specific historical occurrences, specific forms—without, however, excluding the influence of lawlike relations from their scope. In a similar manner, even the historical disciplines among the natural sciences are interested in unique processes and forms. Indeed, the concept of a gestalt

---

2. The set-theoretical paradoxes which arise with the idea of an encompassing whole as the "set of all sets" may be linked with this phenomenon: the "set of all sets" would have to include itself as a member (subset), since one does not distinguish between sets qualitatively but only according to different quantities of homogeneous elements. The homogenization of space and time has as a consequence the abstraction from qualitatively different entities.

or of form in general stands in the middle between the concept of law found in the natural sciences and the interest in individual life-forms discernible in history and philology. The notion of form can characterize what is peculiar to the individual as well as what is typical, and is therefore especially important for biology (A. Portmann). Yet the interest in individual gestalts of life need not imply any vitalistic reservations against applying the general methods and ways of observing found in the natural sciences to life appearances. Still, the most consistent application of such methods within the realm of biology will not obscure the fact that they are employed there in the service of a different constellation of problems than is the case within classical mechanics or modern field theory.

The interest of the human sciences in individual appearances does not affect the validity of the results that the natural sciences or other nomological sciences obtain when they are applied to the phenomena encountered in the study of history and literature. Nonetheless, since the nomological sciences presuppose the equal validity (and thus indifference) of all individual appearances, that aspect of reality which forms the actual theme of the historico-philological disciplines tends to disappear under their perspective. By contrast, the category of the whole, with its interest in what is individual, can be shown to be the leading category in the consciousness of the human sciences. In the first place, every individual is a whole. Moreover, every individual appearance occurs within a context which itself is unique, and which itself forms (in a certain sense) a whole in which the individual appearance has a specific, unexchangeable place. For precisely this reason, each appearance is part of such a whole.

Paradigmatic for such relationships is the position of the individual word in the sentence, and of the sentence within both the context of a discourse or segment of text and the context of the situation in which it was originally formulated.

It is possible to progress along both of these lines from smaller to larger totalities: from the individual segment of discourse to the whole of the discourse or the work in question, and on to its place within the oeuvre of its author; or from the situation of the individual sentence and the individual discourse to the whole of the social world and, finally, of the cultural epoch in which they are located. From these comments it can be seen that the whole in its significance for the so-called human sciences is essentially a *semantic* whole, within which various levels of meaning totalities are to be differentiated, levels which are again related to one another as parts and wholes. Consequently, it is not only in the study of literature and philology but also in history that the subject matter must be characterized as a meaning whole at each level of analysis.

*   *   *

It has become clear in the discussion up to this point that the category of the whole and its parts is of fundamental significance for the so-called human sciences and their methodology. It is thus not a specialized or exclusively theological category. We can only describe the significance of this category for theology, then, as a modification of the role which it plays within the whole realm of those sciences that are concerned with what is *individual*. It is no coincidence that here we are concerned above all with the realm of the realities of human life, since it is precisely with respect to humans that what is individual strikes us as relevant, as being of general interest (to put it paradoxically). No doubt this is associated with the fact that we ourselves are human individuals.

The connection of theology and the human sciences is established for Christian theology through the fact that God became man. This means that Christian theology conceives the reality of God as present for our world in a specific human history, namely, in the history of Jesus of Nazareth. Consequently, theology will of necessity occupy itself with the traditions stemming from this historical individual: with the process of their exposition, with the disparity of the times, yet also with the context of the Jewish religion and its authoritative documents, which in turn must be evaluated in connection with the history of human religions and of human history *in toto*. Not of least importance, Christian theology is concerned with the problems which these factors raise for the question of the present relevance and truth of the history and person of Jesus. Throughout, they are problems of the same kind as occur in the human sciences. Thus we find that the category "part/whole" plays a similar role for theological hermeneutics in the matter of textual interpretation as it does for the other literary-historical disciplines. In research into the events of early Christianity, ancient Israel, or the history of the Church, this category bears the same significance as in the profane historical disciplines, since the significance of any individual occurrence must be understood within its larger context or contexts. But the individual case is also critically illuminated by the broader context, even to the point of a return inquiry into the facticity of the occurrence as alleged by the tradition.

For theology, the category of the whole has still another specific significance above and beyond this meaning. It is not only within theology that the categorical structure which is foundational for all the human sciences undergoes a modification. Already in historical studies an application of the category of the whole occupies the foreground, an application that is different from the one in the study of literature. In literary studies, the interpretation of a text involves inquiring into the significance of the words within the context of the sentence and of the sentence in the context of the discourse. The whole that constitutes the object of interpretation appears here in the guise of a text, even when, as is the case in historical-critical interpretation, the text is classified within an historical context.

By contrast, in history we are concerned with processes in which the significance of individual appearances changes with time. The whole that is the object of historical examination has essentially the character of a process. This is true for an individual biography and for the history of an institution, society, or entire epoch, as well as for the representation of any specific individual process that forms a definable unit within the broader context—a unit such as the history of Solomon's successors on the throne of David, for example. Texts are not the subject matter in such historical inquiries; they are only the material, the resources for reconstructing the process in question. The process itself is the whole of its parts and, as a whole, will only come into view from the end, when it has run its course. For instance, the historian cannot speak of the Thirty Years' War in Germany or make it the object of his study until these thirty years have passed. Anyone who would have spoken before 1648 of the Thirty Years' War with reference to that series of events would not have been an historian but a prophet. Yet, insofar as the completed processes to which the historian's interest turns always stand in the context of more encompassing, not yet completed processes, the judgments of the historian can never be completely cleansed from some admixture of the prophetic.

Theological exegesis and theological accounts of history are subject to more rigorous demands, even after maximal assimilation of the general methods of the human sciences. Perhaps the expositor of Plato or Goethe can ignore the question of what relevance her subject has for the present— even though her own interest already suggests some such relevance. But the expositor of the Gospel of John or the Pauline letters cannot afford to do so if she wants to do any justice at all in her exegesis to the definitiveness that the texts themselves claim. Indeed, even the historian of Israel or of the Christian Church will find it difficult to neglect the spe-

cific claim to truth which is tied to these historical phenomena. The same also applies, by the way, to the treatment of
other religious traditions, especially those whose claim to
truth extends, as does that of the Jewish religion and Christianity, to the whole of humanity.

The particular significance which the category of the
whole holds for theology (and continues to hold, even when
the individual theologian shies· away from taking this fact
into account) is conditioned by the idea of God. Whoever uses
the word "God," particularly as a singular, makes a claim at
the same time about the totality of what exists finitely. The
Christian doctrine of God as the Creator of the world has this
significance. Moreover, God's sending of Jesus Christ is concerned, at least according to its intention, with the reconcilia-
tion and redemption of the entire world. Without this reference to the totality of what exists finitely in the world, a
reference that we find also within eschatology in the concept
of the universal judgment and a new heaven and earth, talk
about God—about the *one* God—would not be possible.
Further, when the connection of theistic language with the
totality of finite reality is not conceived in the light of these
implications, talk of God becomes empty and thoughtless,
reduced finally to an unnecessary and bothersome ballast
from which we would prefer to free ourselves.

The concept of the whole as the all-inclusive whole of
all finite reality, a notion that in the human sciences otherwise
remains nebulously in the background, therefore becomes an
explicit theme for theology whether one wishes it or not. In
contradistinction to the metaphysical tradition within philosophy, however, the totality of the world is certainly not the
real theme for theology, but only the correlate of its real
theme, the idea of God. God is not the whole of what exists
finitely, and the concept of the whole does not include God
within it as one of its parts. Whatever is a part of the whole—
a part alongside other such parts and in distinction to the
whole—is for that reason finite (in the sense of the Hegelian

definition of the finite as a something in distinction to an other) and thus cannot be God.

But neither can the whole be absolute, and therefore it cannot be God—at least not if it, as the whole of its parts, not only itself constitutes the being-as-part of its parts, but conversely is also dependent on the parts whose whole it is. This means that the whole cannot be conceptualized as self-constitutive. As the whole of its parts, it is a unified unity that presupposes some ground of itself as *unifying unity*. As the unifying unity of the world, God is distinct from the totality of the finite, though again not absolutely distinct. If God were merely distinct in relation to the totality of the finite, then he himself would be finite and would consequently have to be conceived as a part of that totality of the finite that we think of as world. As the unifying unity of the totality of the finite, God is indeed necessarily distinct from it. Yet at the same time, he is just as necessarily immanent to the world of the finite (given that its existence is already presupposed) as the continuing condition of its unity. He is this condition either as the ground of this unity, which then independently continues to exist, or as the force which continuously effects the unity of the parts and thereby remains immanent to the world of the finite and present to its parts.

As long as the unifying unity of the world is only conceived as the unifying force which joins together pre-existing elements into parts of a whole, however, it is only partially conceived as the source of the world: God so conceived would once again be finite, conditioned by an other outside of himself. The infinity of the unifying unity (and so also its difference from that which as finite is *eo ipso* a part of the world as unified unity) can only be maintained if it is not only the source of the unity of the parts but also the source of the parts themselves. Only in this manner would God be conceived as the creative source of the world. In addition, the relationship of God to the world can only be conceived as its creative source under the further condition that the structure of the totality of the world as the whole of its parts is again grounded in God. This structure must be based upon a difference within God, one which typifies the relationship of part and whole but which is not identical with it, for otherwise the life within God would only be a mirror image of the unity of the whole of the world in its parts.

The retrogression from the idea of the whole of the world to the view of God as its unifying unity cannot claim the stringency of a proof of God in the form presented here, for two reasons. First, the argumentation sketched here rests upon the presupposition that the whole of the finite world is not unconditioned as the whole of its parts but itself is also conditioned by the parts. This presupposition, in some tension with the notion of a whole, attributes to the parts a certain independence over against the whole. We will return to this issue below. Second, the concept of unity is one of the most general and therefore most empty categories (category in the sense of Hegelian logic; in the sense of the Aristotelian tradition, the concept of the One would be viewed, because of its inseparability from what truly is [des Seienden], as actually surpassing all categories on account of its generality). Because of this empty generality, the concept of the One is not fit to describe appropriately the differentiated structure that is intended by the expression "God." This became manifest already in the fact that the concept of unity had to be made concrete by means of additions—that is, by means of the moment of activity (as the unifying, as opposed to the unified, unity), as well as through concepts such as "ground" or "force"—in order to express more exactly the relationship of the unifying to the unified unity. Yet even these concepts are not sufficient to express appropriately what is meant by the word "God," as some reflection upon their scope would quickly reveal.

What then is the value in describing the relationship of God and the world by means of such an empty and abstract concept as that of unity? The value of such a description lies in its ability to provide a preliminary characterization, one that allows us to relate the word "God" to the concept of the world as the whole of all finite things without in other respects prejudging the controversial question of the peculiar meaning of the word "God." The concept of unity outlines only the dimension in which this question becomes discussable, since now the word "God" no longer stands without conceptual relationship next to the concept of world. The notion of unity is clearly suited to express this relationship in the most unprejudicial manner because of its extreme generality and emptiness. At the same time, a task for our further reflection is posed by the contrast of God and world as unifying and unified unity, namely, to develop an idea of God which, as unifying unity of the world, can be conceived coherently without losing God's distinction from the world in the process.

Examples of the more explicit determination of the idea of God—activity, ground, force—have already been mentioned, as has the fact that each of these designations in turn is found, upon deeper reflection, to be inadequate, to be only partially relevant. It remains, then, to show that we cannot by this means expect any final answer to the question of the reality of God. Assuredly, discourse about God will always employ representations and concepts. Even the word "God" itself as a general expression within language is subject to this rule. The concrete structure of the divine life in its individuality cannot yet again be characterized categorically (i.e., using an abstract aspect of some totality) in the belief that such expressions as "Concept" or "Idea" would appropriately describe the individuality of the divine reality. Such attempts neglect what has already been described as the peculiarity of God in relationship to the totality of the finite—though they may do this just because it is problematic, not because they feel the problem has been solved. The idea of God is destroyed when he is conceived as an application instance (even though it be the highest instance) of some general structure which in its generality is distinct from God and which is asserted as a predicate of God.

But if God must be distinguished from the totality of the finite, what significance still remains for the category of part and whole within theology? In reflection on the most comprehensive whole of all finite reality, each particular finite thing in its concrete, individual definiteness is mediated with God. For this reason, religion as a vivid and deeper apprehension of reality consists, as Schleiermacher saw, in the becoming conscious of the infinite and whole in the individual and finite, a whole out of which each individual thing is, as it were, carved by means of its definition and its determination. Correspondingly, theology is able, by means of reflection on the totality of finite reality as the horizon of meaning of all individual existence, to show its relatedness to the reality of God.

This applies also to christology: Only through the relation to the whole of humanity in its history, only through the eschatological import of his appearing and his history, can the unity of Jesus with God be expressed. This unity announces conversely (from God's perspective) that God was incarnate in this person. Through this relation to the whole of humanity in its history, the relation of each human life to the God revealed in Jesus is disclosed in the light of the history of Jesus as the new Adam. No objection to this position can be based upon the observation that history is not present as a completed whole, that its process is, on the contrary, incomplete. Moreover, it remains true that the actual process of history devours individuals and empires rather than bringing them to harmonious completion as parts of a meaning-whole. We already saw that historical hermeneutics diverges from that of literature in this respect. Individuals are caught up and snatched away in the process of their history; but Jesus, in bringing close to them the meaning that is tied up with their wholeness, discloses to them their salvation within a history that is not yet complete.

The category of the whole (and its relationship to the parts) therefore has its specific significance for theology in that it makes possible the conceptual mediation between the

146

finite and the absolute reality of God. The justification for this mediation is ultimately grounded in the fact that God himself mediates his creation with himself through the process of history. The concept of the whole is related to this process in a general and thus abstract manner, but one which discloses at the same time the methodology for understanding its concrete, individual moments. Because of its abstractness, the answer to the question of the true form of the divine reality cannot be derived from the concept of the whole alone. Yet its methodological fruitfulness stems from just this abstractness, since it yields a general description of a field of possible experiences and inquiries without prejudicing their concrete solutions.

*　　　*　　　*

The similarities and differences in the preceding comments to certain of Hegel's formulations in his *Science of Logic* make it necessary to take an explicit position concerning Hegel's interpretation and classification of the categories whole and part. In Hegel's *Logic* the category of the whole appears as a step in the process of reflection, one which leads to the overcoming of the opposition of essence and mere being. This opposition arises in the second book of the *Logic* with the introduction of the Concept of Essence, over against which being is degraded to mere show [*Schein*]. The overcoming of this opposition does not succeed until its two sides are conceived as belonging together in such a manner that their identity is conceived in their difference. According to Hegel, the overcoming does not occur with the concept of the whole, because this concept has its truth in the parts out of which the whole is composed. In his discussion Hegel treats the concept of the whole under the viewpoint of the essential relation, in which the two sides belong essentially together. He discerns its immediate form in the relationship of whole and parts: the

147

parts are essential to the whole, just as, conversely, the whole is essential to the parts. But Hegel then moves on to other, (presumably) logically higher forms of this reciprocity, namely, Force and its Expression, and Outer and Inner. In this manner he attains in his larger *Logic* to the notion of the Absolute. The Absolute, though, is still determined by the connection to an other as it becomes visible in the relation of substance and accidence, of cause and effect, and finally in the structure of reciprocity. It is only the concept of Concept [*Begriff*] which contains in itself as its own moments both sides of essence and appearance as the universal and the particular, together with their unity in the individual.

Yet it appears that Hegel treated the notion of the whole one-sidedly by classifying it under the viewpoint of the essential relation, that is, by one-sidedly emphasizing the duality and reciprocity of whole and parts. In doing so, he did not do full justice to the inequality of the two sides of this conceptual relationship. Admittedly, Hegel emphasizes that parts and whole mutually imply and condition one another,[3] yet he neglects their logical imbalance. The relation to the whole as something different from and exceeding the part is indeed posited in the concept of a part, but in the concept of the whole the parts are posited not as other, but as the whole's own moments. In a certain sense Hegel also draws attention to this distinction by placing "the immediate self-subsistence" of the parts and the "reflected self-subsistence" of the whole in contrast to one another.[4] However, if this distinction means that the whole is not posited in the parts, but rather that the

---

3. *Hegel's Science of Logic,* trans. A. V. Miller (London: George Allen and Unwin; New York: Humanities Press, 1969), p. 515. German edition: *Wissenschaft der Logik,* 2 vols., ed. George Lasson, Philosophische Bibliothek, vols. 56-57 (Leipzig: Felix Meiner, 1923), 2:140. [References to the German edition will be given in parentheses.—TRANS.]

4. Ibid., pp. 513-14 (138-39); cf. pp. 515-16 (141).

parts are invariably posited in the reflected unity of the whole as inner moments of its concept, then one can no longer say that the whole "is indifferent to the parts."[5] If one views the parts as "the self-subsistent substrate," over against which the whole would be "only an external relation,"[6] then one has already ceased to look at the parts as parts. Such a way of viewing the problem has already lost the idea of the whole and is no longer able to describe the "in itself manifold existence" as a plurality of parts whose concept already presupposes that of the whole. When this happens, it is no longer correct to speak of a "self-subsistence of the sides"[7] in the relationship of the whole and the parts.

In the concept of the whole as a whole of parts, therefore, the "other" of the whole, the part, is already posited as an inner element. To be sure, the *particularization* of the parts as the inner elements of the whole cannot be understood simply from the general concept of the whole as such. For this reason, the parts are indeed the immediate form in which the whole represents itself. The underivability of the parts from the general concept of a whole hinders us from thinking of the concept of the whole as self-constituting and thus absolute. This does not change the fact, however, that the elements of content which are linked to the whole form its parts only as elements of this whole and, insofar as they are parts, do not possess any logical independence over against the concept of the whole.

The situation is quite different in the case of the relationship between the categories of Force and its Expression, between Inner and Outer, and even that between substance and accidence: force must express itself, but the expression is not the force; the inner is the inner of an outer side that belongs to it but is not the inner; nor are the accidents the substance or the effects the cause. By contrast, the parts are

---

5. So, ibid., p. 516 (141).
6. Ibid., p. 514 (139).
7. Ibid.

in fact the whole, since the whole as the whole of its parts is, in its parts, only what it is according to its concept. The concept of the whole, in the sense of the Hegelian logic itself, thus appears to be a richer, more differentiated category than that of Force or the Inner, as well as logically richer than substance and causality. For this reason one must doubt whether the classification of this category within the course of the Hegelian logic is a correct one.

Such doubts are confirmed through the observation that Hegel himself in fact utilizes the concept "totality," but also the concept of the whole, as a category of a higher order than one would be led to presume by his presentation in the *Logic*.[8] This is apparent in his famous sentence: "The true is the whole. The whole, however, is merely the essential nature reaching its completeness through the process of its development."[9] Even in the *Logic* itself, one finds statements in which the concept of the whole functions in a similar, less unpretentious manner. Thus the Concept is characterized as "the whole itself," as the "posited unity of itself in its determinations."[10] The "Logic" in the *Encyclopedia* of 1817 names the Object, as the realization of the Concept, the "whole" or the "totality of the Concept,"[11] whereby the expressions "whole" and "totality" stand parallel to one another. This is even more clearly the

---

8. Lorenz Puntel has brought to my attention that similar questions arise as well in the case of other of Hegel's logical categories. An especially clear example is the concept of the Absolute (*Logic*, pp. 530ff. [2:157ff.]), which in the "Logic" of the *Encyclopedia* is no longer treated at this place (*Encyclopedia*, § 142). The concept of the Infinite, which Hegel assigned a very elementary level in the "Logic of Being," also plays in his linguistic usage a much more significant role than one would expect from its classification in the course of the *Logic*.

9. Hegel, *The Phenomenology of Mind*, trans. J. B. Baillie (New York: Harper & Row, 1967), p. 81. German edition: *Phänomenologie des Geistes*, ed. Johannes Hoffmeister, Philosophische Bibliothek, vol. 114 (Hamburg: Felix Meiner, 1952), p. 21.

10. *Logic*, p. 555 (2:185).

11. *Encyclopedia*, § 193.

case in the larger *Logic*, when Hegel says of Mechanism that it shows itself to be "a striving for totality in the fact that it seeks to grasp nature by itself as a *whole* which, for its concept, does not require any other."[12] This more specific characterization of the whole—that it does not require any other for its concept—is at the same time the realization of its concept.

When at the conclusion of the *Logic* Hegel finally says of the logical science that it is "itself the pure Concept which . . . in running itself as subject matter through the totality of its determinations, develops itself into the whole of its reality, into the system of science,"[13] the parallelism of the expressions "whole" and "totality" once again reveals that no set terminological difference can be assumed between these two expressions as used by Hegel. When Hegel distinguishes two "totalities" in the transition from his dialectic of appearance to the chapter on the essential relation, namely, the manifested and the essential world[14]—the difference of whole and part corresponds to this distinction in what follows—this does not mean that the concept of totality has a broader scope than that of the whole. It might appear so, since the concept of the whole stands for only one of the two totalities in the comments that follow. But instead, with the appearance of these two totalities the concept of totality or of the "whole" itself becomes dialectical: each of the two sides is in itself at the same time the "whole" of the relationship.[15] Hegel says this expressly in the introduction to the chapter on the absolute relation: the sides of this relation are "totalities," because in their difference they are appearances or "show" [*Schein*], "for as show the differences are themselves and their opposite, or [they are] the whole."[16] Accordingly, if there is

---

12. *Logic*, p. 736 (2:386).
13. Ibid., p. 843 (2:505).
14. Ibid., p. 511 (2:136).
15. Ibid., p. 512 (2:137).
16. Ibid., p. 554 (2:185).

no set terminological difference between the expressions "whole" and "totality" in Hegel, then it clearly follows from the usage of the term "totality" (which occurs much more frequently in Hegel than "whole") that the function of the concept of the whole in Hegel extends far beyond the subordinate role that he assigned to it in the presentation of the logical determinations. The concept of the whole or the totality functions much more in Hegel's own thought de facto as the category of categories, as the integral of their abstract particularity.

To be sure, Hegel wished, above and beyond the abstract concept of the whole, to think the concrete whole itself using the concept of the Idea, and to do so on the basis of the principle that constitutes it, which in the process of realizing simultaneously realizes itself. Using this concept of the Idea, Hegel also eliminated the difference between God and world, thereby replacing the concept of God with that of the absolute Idea. Yet has not the abstract thereby been passed off as the concrete, despite all his efforts to the contrary, in that the world is represented as the product of the logical concept which releases Nature out of itself? In opposition to such a view, the position here presented insists upon the abstractness of every concept of the whole or of the totality, an abstractness that results from the anticipatory nature of all knowledge of the whole in a world which has not yet been completed and reconciled to the whole. To this corresponds the consciousness of the difference of the world from God— a difference which, to be sure, must not be hardened into a dualism, since this would result in making God himself finite, yet one which also, as the condition of the unity of any creature with God, will not be transcended and eliminated even in the eschaton.

CHAPTER 8

MEANING, RELIGION, AND THE QUESTION OF GOD

A MEANINGFUL LIFE is no longer taken for granted in the modern world. The concern with emptiness and loss of meaning, together with a questioning about and searching after meaning, has become a predominant theme in our time. As early as 1925, Paul Tillich suggested that the question of meaning has attained as fundamental a significance for modern folk as the question of overcoming transitoriness had for people of antiquity and the striving for forgiveness from sin had in the medieval world. For Tillich, all individual meaning is dependent on an unconditioned "ground of meaning," which both surpasses and serves as foundation for the totality of all individual semantic (meaning-related) contents.[1] In a largely similar manner, Viktor Frankl has spoken since the Second World War of an "unconditional meaning" [*Über-Sinn*] which grounds that meaning of existence without which humans could not exist.[2] Like Tillich, Frankl perceives

---

1. Paul Tillich, "The Philosophy of Religion," in *What Is Religion?* ed. James Luther Adams (New York: Harper & Row, 1969), chap. 1. German edition: *Religionsphilosophie* (1925); republished in an Urban-Reihe edition, vol. 63 (1962), pp. 42, 44ff.

2. Viktor E. Frankl, *The Will to Meaning: Foundations and Applica-*

clearly that one is concerned here in the final analysis with the religious quest. Nevertheless, in the experience of the "lack of meaning," that malady of our times is visible which stems from our secular society's disregard for God and which according to Frankl provides the explanation for the dramatic rise in the number of neurotic illnesses and especially of suicides.

All such inquiries into meaning are concerned with what it is to possess meaning, that is, with the possibility of a life that even in suffering could be experienced and affirmed as meaningful. The meaning-filled life cannot be presupposed or taken for granted, as the experiences of emptiness and meaninglessness demonstrate clearly enough. From this observation many assume that we must create our own meaning and thus impart meaning to a reality that appears meaningless. Indeed, this view is dominant in contemporary sociology of knowledge under the influence of Husserl, Alfred Schütz, and Theodor Lessing. Thus, for Peter Berger the human formation of culture is fundamentally a matter of the creation of meaning; similarly, Niklas Luhmann views "the overcoming of contingence" as the most foundational accomplishment of a social system. From here it is only a short step to viewing the overcoming of experienced meaninglessness also for the *individual* as a task which involves a human creation of meaning. Solving the problem would then only depend on finding the power to give meaning to one's own life, in order to extricate oneself from the crippling influence of the Medusan countenance of meaninglessness.

But is the experience of meaning a matter of creating meaning or of discovering an already given meaning? In order to pursue this question, it is necessary to distinguish a

tions of Logotherapy (New York: New American Library, Plume Books, 1969), p. 156. German edition: *Der Wille zum Sinn* (1972), p. 117. The book stems from a series of lectures at the Perkins School of Theology, Southern Methodist University, Dallas, Texas, summer 1966.

formal concept of meaning from that of the meaning-filled life. The formal concept is more comprehensive than the actually meaningful. For example, the experience of the *absence* of meaning is also semantically structured and thus not devoid of meaning; the same pertains as well to the nihilistic denial of a meaningful world. Indeed, it is only because of the semantic or meaning-related structure of language that one can even articulate the conviction of the meaninglessness of life.

The distinction of a formal notion of what it is to be meaningful from actual meaning-filled content (Gerhard Sauter) is suggested to us also by a study of what is contained in the sentences of a discourse or text and which is grasped linguistically. This type of meaning is concerned with the meaning of the words in a sentence and of the sentences in the context of a discourse. The individual words have their meaning not only as designations for objects and states of affairs but also through their positions in the sentence.

Thinkers have attempted to draw a neat distinction between the two concepts "meaning" [*Bedeutung*] and "sense" [*Sinn*]. For instance, Frege spoke of the meaning of the words as names for objects, and opposed this concept to the sense of the sentence as a whole. In his view sense has to do with the whole within which the words are arranged as components of the sentence. Now, it may as a matter of fact be the case that the concept of "sense" does belong primarily to sentences and that of "meaning" to words. However, the words have their meanings initially within sentences, and this meaning is not completely separable from the context of an individual sentence. A sentence is not merely a mechanical construction of words whose meanings are already set. Rather, the individual word, taken alone, always bears a certain degree of indeterminacy. It is no coincidence that dictionaries offer various nuances of meaning for each word, nuances which are abstracted from the word's actual use in sentences.

In a sentence the individual word receives a higher degree of semantic determinacy. This is because in a sentence the word bears meaning in a second sense, namely, as a constituent of the sentence. Here we normally speak of the *sense* of the word within the context of the sentence. It is not only the sentence as a whole that has a sense but also its individual constituents, the individual words: in the words the sense of the sentence is articulated. Thus, sense and meaning belong together; they resist a neat assignment to sentences and words. It is especially important, though, to differentiate two aspects within the notion of the word "meaning" itself: the reference to an object, and the position of the individual word in the sentence. Since meaning has to do with the position of particulars within the context of the whole, it is thus possible to speak also of the meaning of the particular sentence within the broader context of a discourse or text.

Linguistic meaning has therefore to do with the relationships between parts and a whole within the context of a discourse. At the same time, however, we are concerned with the subject which is being spoken about and which is "represented" through the mediation of the meanings of the words that make up the sentence. Now, of course, language has not only a representational function but expressive and communicative functions as well. There are forms of linguistic expression in which these other functions occupy the foreground. Nonetheless, the representational function always plays a part and may in turn move to the fore, namely, in the case of assertorial sentences. Assertions claim to be true in the sense that the meaning of such sentences attempts to represent an objectively existing meaning, a state of affairs. It is this truth claim which constitutes the sense or import of such sentences qua assertions.

Does the sense that linguistic utterances have owe its existence to a human bestowal of meaning? At first glance, this appears indeed to be the case. Sentences are, for example, spoken *by us,* leading us to think that their meaning is the result of our efforts. Since meaning can only be grasped linguistically, the belief that language is the product of human activity suggests to us that we might view all meaning as the product of a human bestowal of meaning. However, if we do so, two factors that are crucial to the semantic structure of linguistic utterances drop from sight.

In the first place, this view fails to consider that it is part of the nature of language itself to represent a reality that is already given, as we saw in our examination of the assertion. Even if only a few assertions are "true," it cannot be the case that all asserted meaning is only the expression of a human bestowal of meaning. True assertions are true precisely in that their content corresponds to the state of affairs that is being asserted. Now, the spoken or written sentence may be the product of a human activity as well; nonetheless, true sentences and true assertions are related to the reality of the asserted state of affairs in the sense of a discovery of meaning rather than in the sense of a bestowal of meaning.

A second important factor is the fact that there are many layers to the meaning of linguistic utterances. A spoken sentence always brings to expression something above and beyond the meaning that the speaker supposed or intended. It is not unusual that we say in reality something different from what we wanted to say. This is only possible insofar as the meaning of a sentence, once it has been spoken, proceeds from the combination of the words themselves, independently of the intentions which the speaker had in speaking it. A sentence can say more than the speaker actually wanted to say. It can also fall short of the thought which she wanted to express and which can be independently inferred from the context of her speech. Finally, a sentence can convey something completely different from what she intended. All of these things are matters of the interpretation of what was said. Moreover, every linguistic expression stands in need of interpretation by the listener or reader.

Nevertheless, interpretations can miss the meaning which the author intended the utterances to have, as well as the meaning which actually should have been derived from what was said. This possibility of error weighs heavily against the view that interpretations are only a bestowal of meaning. If the interpretation can miss the meaning of its object, then the meaning of a sentence, a discourse, or a text is obviously not merely dependent on the interpreter. Nevertheless, as we saw, meaning does not depend only on the speaker or author of the text. For these reasons, the semantic structure of the texts that we interpret appears to be an independent entity, and the appropriateness or inappropriateness of interpretations must be judged in relation to it.

In a similar manner, assertions also presuppose rather than produce the meaning of the corresponding state of affairs. Assertorial sentences rely unavoidably upon the meaning structures of states of affairs, which are prior to human perception and its articulation in language. Meaning can be approached through language but it is not the product of language. Otherwise, all speaking with assertorial sentences would be misguided. If the use of assertions is meaningful—that is, if they express the particular nature of human experience and experienced reality—then reality must be somehow meaningfully structured prior to its being grasped in language, even if language is the only way to articulate this meaning structure. Language can either grasp or miss the semantic structure of reality, and therefore this semantic structure is not first created through language. To reduce meaning to language is to take the first step along a path which culminates in the position that all meaning is merely created through human action—that is, that it is the product of a bestowal of meaning.

Yet this position falsifies the actual state of affairs by reversing the actual priority. In fact, human action is itself dependent on perceptions of meaning, since there is no action without goal setting, which requires the choice of the means relevant to a given goal. This process always presupposes an orientation to the world and the grasp of semantic content. Now, a perceptive grasp of semantic content is admittedly itself an activity [*Tätigkeit*], but it is not an action [*Handeln*]; it does not realize self-chosen ends through the use of means. Nor is speaking and the grasp of reality through language— contrary to the prejudgments of contemporary speech act theories—always an action. We form verbal utterances only secondarily, as means for the attainment of selected goals or as ends in themselves; in both these special cases they are moments of an action. But that is not the fundamental character of spoken language.

This criticism of the reduction of linguistically grasped meaning to acts of human meaning bestowal is of fundamental significance for our theme. The connection of religion and the experience of meaning can only be conceptualized appropriately if the experienced meaning is seen to precede its comprehension by humans rather than being understood solely as the product of a human bestowal of meaning. If the latter were the case, religion would be merely a human projection, lacking any truth content that surpasses the human consciousness. But we have seen that the reduction of the perception and comprehension of meaning to a bestowal of meaning pulls the ground out from under the very notion of the truth of assertions themselves, not only from the truth claims of religious statements.

The connection between religion and the experience of meaning becomes visible when one turns from the meaning-structures of linguistic utterances to the way in which human experiencing [*Erleben*] can be meaningful. Human experiencing is a special case of the semantic structure of reality itself, which we must consider as preceding its linguistic representation. Experiencing has to do with the ontological structure of a creature who is capable of language, and thus with the social context within which language is developed and used. In this phenomenon, the foundation of linguistically articulated meaning in prelinguistic meaning structure is perceptible in a special way.

We owe the first foundational analyses of the experience of meaning to Wilhelm Dilthey, who dealt with the semantic structures of experiencing in his late notes and sketches, which in turn formed the starting point for Heidegger's analyses of individual human existence [*Dasein*]. Dilthey transformed the discussion of words in context to an inquiry into the structure of experiencing. He did not explicitly discuss this transition, since he presupposed that the meaning structures found in language themselves were only the expression of the meaning relatedness of the psychic life. For this reason Dilthey believed that it was possible to speak about meaning and meaning relationships only in the realm of the *psyche*.

For us, however, the transition from linguistic meaning to the postulation of a semantic structure to prelinguistic reality requires a justification that can only be obtained through observations of language itself. In the foregoing argumentation, we have appealed to the representational function of language, and particularly to the structure of assertions, to justify the supposition of structures of meaning that extend beyond the realm of the linguistic. In so doing, we have defended a much more extensive acceptance of semantic structures than did Dilthey, who limited them to the realm of the psychic life. In contrast to his position, we may now expect, in *all* realms of reality, that particular appearances can be understood as parts of more complete meaning-forms [*Sinngestalten*]—that is, contexts of meaning in Dilthey's sense exist everywhere, even beyond the realm of the phenomena of organic and psychic life.

Although I have argued for a wider context, Dilthey's special case of the human life-context does carry particular significance for the perception of meaning, since for humans the whole of their lives is present at every moment along with the particulars of their own experiencing. Dilthey, at any rate, expressed it in this way with his concept of experiencing. An individual event becomes an experience to the extent that it is grasped as one specific articulation of a whole life. Perhaps Dilthey construed the notion of experience too narrowly by relating it only to the whole of the individual life.

Heidegger's analysis of Dasein in *Being and Time* suffers from the same shortcoming. We have no specific consciousness of the whole of our own life (in contradistinction to all else) at the moment of immediate experiencing. Much more, it is the whole of reality itself that is present to us in feeling, not only the whole of our own life. In such a vague presence of reality itself, world, self, and God are as yet undifferentiated. The whole has definiteness only in the particular experience. The individual occasion of experiencing, though, is not just something particular; in it, the whole of reality appears—just as the meaning-context of a discourse appears in the individual words and sentences. In experiencing, the whole of reality is not fully contained in the individual experience; there remains a vague element of "above and beyond," which at the same time forms the framework in which the individual experience can first become what it is. There is—as modern philosophy since Descartes has seen, and as medieval Scholastic thought already knew—a vague awareness of an undetermined infinite which always precedes all comprehension of anything finite or determined. As Descartes said, the finite can only be comprehended as a limitation of this infinite.

This, then, is the background of Dilthey's concept of experiencing. Dilthey may have identified himself more with Schleiermacher and Spinoza than with Descartes, but in this matter Spinoza was only a student of Descartes. Dilthey narrowed the horizon of the undetermined infinite and whole, which is present to us in our affections as the horizon of our individual experiences, to the totality of life—indeed, of the individual's own life. He gained thereby the basis for centering his philosophy on the concept of life [*Lebensphilosophie*] and for his descriptions of the ontological structure of experiencing, as well as for his view of the human experience of the self as a process of self-interpretation. Under this view, as a life history progresses the meaning structures of earlier experiences shift, because the whole of life appears again and again under new perspectives, that is, from the viewpoint of new experiences. What was earlier experienced as important becomes unimportant, and other scarcely noticed moments of earlier experiencing can increase in significance. Thus Dilthey writes: "Not until the last moment of a life can the final estimate of its meaning be made."[3] Until then, the meaning of the particular moments of experiencing shifts, as does the meaning of the whole of one's life. Herein lies the finitude of our knowledge about life as a whole. We can never attain a comprehensive overview of the total meaning of our life—not because we have absolutely no relationship to our life as a whole, but because we always have such a relationship to our life and to life in general only from the limited viewpoint of a specific experience, from which we remember earlier experiences and await future ones. This viewpoint changes as our personal history progresses through time. Consequently, we possess the whole, the total meaning of life, only in the manner in which it is represented in the respective individual experiences.

It is amazing to note how closely this description of the semantic structure of experiencing in Dilthey's thought is connected with Schleiermacher's description of religious experience in the second of his *Speeches* (1799). In that work religious experience is an intuition [*Anschauung*] of the infinite and whole in one individual, finite content. We come to such a view of the universe when we become cognizant that what is individual and finite does not exist for itself but rather is "cut out," together with its boundaries which constitute its

---

3. Wilhelm Dilthey, *Gesammelte Schriften*, 16 vols. in 18, ed. Bernhard Groethuysen (Leipzig: Tübner, and Göttingen: Vandenhoeck & Ruprecht, 1914-72), 7:237.

particularity, of the infinite and the whole. In point of fact, this is the same conception which we can find already in Descartes, that we can only comprehend finite objects through a circumscription of the infinite. We are, however—as Schleiermacher further points out—normally not aware of this fact in our everyday lives, interacting as we do with finite objects and states of affairs as if they had their existence from and in themselves. It is only in the higher awareness of religious experiences that we become aware of the actual, deeper reality of things, namely, that they are constituted by and through the "universe," that is, the infinite and the whole. According to Schleiermacher, this higher perceptual awareness constitutes the unique essence of religious experience. Yet even religious awareness can grasp the universe only through intuitions of finite things and states of affairs. For this reason, Schleiermacher allows for an indefinite multiplicity of various forms of religious consciousness according to the character of the particular intuition by means of which the universe is comprehended, since each intuition is seen as a part of the whole and thus as a revelation of the whole.

Here is the point of contact with Dilthey. We "have" the whole of life, its total meaning, only in the individual and the specific, in which the whole manifests itself. Now, human experience can attain unity in the midst of the multiplicity of impressions and intuitions by means of a ruling or guiding intuition to which everything else is related. But even when one such integrating intuition becomes dominant—a phenomenon which, according to Schleiermacher, underlies individual religious life histories as well as the origin and development of the historical religions—this intuition still remains bound to a particular viewpoint, in a manner similar to Dilthey's position concerning the experience or significance of one's own life.

Perhaps Dilthey highlighted the historicity of this process more strongly than Schleiermacher. For example, he speaks of the possibility of a final knowledge of the meaning of our existence at the end of our life (or, in the case of the history of humanity, at the end of history itself). However, this eschatological possibility of a final decision about the meaning of life and of its individual moments must actually lie at some point beyond life, since a life is over at its "last moment." For Dilthey, occasional comments like these function only to underscore the point that a final knowledge of the total meaning of life is inaccessible—and in this matter he is in complete agreement with Schleiermacher.

Of course, Dilthey's closeness to Schleiermacher here is not coincidental: he occupied himself intensely with Schleiermacher's thought for decades, and a major biography of Schleiermacher belongs among Dilthey's chief works. It is thus not surprising that Dilthey was also influenced by Schleiermacher in his systematic thought. As we saw, he followed Schleiermacher's understanding of the finiteness and particularity of our awareness of the whole of life. In opposition to Hegel, who believed it possible to comprehend the infinite whole unbrokenly in the form of Idea, Dilthey also appropriated Schleiermacher's view of the relativity of this awareness to specific experiences within one's own history.

This awareness—that we have the whole only in and through the fragments—links Dilthey to Schleiermacher. Yet for Dilthey the whole is conceptualized differently than for Schleiermacher: it no longer connotes the universe of reality itself, but rather the whole of "life" in the process of its history. The shift has its basis in Dilthey's limitation of the concept of meaning to life, as we saw above. Tied to this limitation is the fact that Dilthey no longer spoke in an explicitly religious manner of the presence of the whole in experiencing but only related this state of affairs to the theme of the experience of the self.

I have dealt with Dilthey in such detail because of the incisive nature of his analyses of the semantic structure of human experiencing, analyses which are fundamental for the contemporary discussion. This is especially true of his position on the significance of individual moments in the context of the whole, a whole which always remains incomplete for the experiencing individuals themselves during the process of their history. Wherever the question of meaning is related to the whole of life and of experienced reality—as, for example, in Tillich's work—such that each individual meaning possesses its significance only from an all-encompassing context of meaning, there Dilthey's analyses can be detected in the background. In Frankl's psychology we also meet up with this understanding of meaning, which is occupied with the relationship of parts of life to the whole and with the presence of this whole in the individual experience. In contrast to Dilthey, Frankl seeks in this way to do more than merely describe the meaning-structure of experiencing. Whereas such a description would leave open the question of whether life is actually experienced as meaningful or as meaningless, Frankl also desires to encourage trust in life's meaningfulness through a total meaning [Gesamtsinn] which encompasses life as a whole, though for him such a total meaning can only be grasped indirectly through the mediation of, and in, concrete life-situations. Once again the semantic structure of experiencing, viewed formally, proves to be linked with the religious theme.

Before we pursue the question of the particularity of the religious awareness of meaning in its relationship to the semantic structuredness of human experiencing generally, we should first emphasize a point which represents perhaps the most important gain provided by Dilthey's analyses of meaning and significance in the context of experiencing. Dilthey's descriptions offer an understanding of meaning and significance according to which these do not stem from a bestowal of meaning by the human subject but proceed from the relationships of life itself, that is, from the relationships of its submoments to the whole of the life-context. Viewed in this way, events already have meaning and significance. This applies also to the events of history, which do not need to have a meaning subsequently conferred upon them through human interpretation. Historical events have meaning and significance themselves according to their contribution to the whole of the life context in which they belong. To be sure, the meaning and significance of the individual events can be determined only relative to the standpoint of historical consciousness.

Dilthey was able, then, through reflection on the historicity of the historical consciousness itself, to do justice to the multiplicity of interpretations of historical occurrences, as well as to the significance which accrues to each but which cannot be fully determined until the end of history. Life's moments have a significance [*Bedeutung*] in themselves, but we can only grasp their significance through the medium of an interpretation [*Deutung*] which itself is conditioned by the perspective of a particular historical standpoint. This insight is valid for the life experience of the individual just as much as for history at large. Only from the end of history could we fully and completely comprehend the significance inherent in the events and forms of history. Only from the end of history, therefore, will a final decision concerning the truth or falsity of our convictions of meaning be made. The evidence which the contemporary experience of meaning provides has the form of faith and of an anticipatory representation of a meaning which has yet to appear with finality.

The relationship between Dilthey's description of the experience of meaning in everyday contexts on the one hand, and the specifically religious consciousness of meaning on the other, has been in principle already elucidated by Schleiermacher. He described the everyday consciousness as oriented toward finite objects and relationships, whereas the religious consciousness comprehends finite realities as grounded in the infinite and whole, thereby intuiting the infinite itself in the finite things. In 1925 Paul Tillich wrote that all individual meaning is conditioned by a context of meaning which in turn rests on an unconditioned ground of meaning. This unconditioned ground of meaning, however, only becomes an explicit topic for the religious consciousness. The cultural consciousness, which is oriented around individual meaning, presupposes such an unconditioned meaning but does not occupy itself expressly with it: "Every cultural act contains the unconditioned meaning; it is based upon the ground of meaning; insofar as it is an act of meaning it is substantially religious." But it is not expressly religious: "Religion is directedness toward the Unconditional, and culture is directedness toward the conditioned forms and their unity."[4]

I gave expression to a similar determination of the relationship of the religious consciousness to the semantic structure of everyday experience in *Theology and the Philosophy of Science*, linking myself more closely than Tillich, however, to the hermeneutical analyses of meaning propounded by Dilthey.[5] I argued there that the religious consciousness has as its explicit theme that totality of meaning which is implicitly presupposed in all everyday experiences of meaning, oriented as they are around individual experiences of significance. Religion has above all to do with the divine reality that grounds and completes the meaning totality of the natural and social world, and thus only indirectly with the totality of meaning of the world itself. Nevertheless, the truth claim made by the religious consciousness must authenticate itself by showing that the God (or gods) alleged by it can actually be understood as the creator and perfecter of the world as in fact experienced. The assertions made by the religious traditions, which are directed beyond formal meaningfulness to the quest for meaning in human life, must

---

4. Tillich, "Philosophy of Religion," p. 59 (= *Religionsphilosophie*, p. 44).

5. See my *Theology and the Philosophy of Science*, trans. Francis McDonagh (Philadelphia: Westminster, 1976).

prove themselves: they must be able to integrate the relations implicit in everyday experiences of meaning within an encompassing context of meaning that grounds all individual meaning. The urgent experiences of senselessness, suffering, and evil are among those life experiences which the religious consciousness of meaning must integrate. If a specific religious tradition is not able to do justice to human experience through such integration, its failure will lead to a crisis of belief in the truth of the tradition; it then becomes questionable whether the God proclaimed by this tradition can, as a matter of fact, be understood as and believed to be the creator and perfecter of the world as actually experienced by humans.

Christian truth claims about God must also face this question of a confirmation through the human experience of meaning and its implications for the understanding of reality as a whole. The feelings, so widespread today, of an all-pervading senselessness, together with the related questioning after meaning, indicate that, for many persons and for broad segments of the public consciousness in our secular culture, the traditional answers of Christianity are no longer adequately functioning as a comprehensive interpretation of the experience of the world's reality and of the life problems that contemporary people face. The individual reasons for this failure cannot be developed here. However, the contemporary question of meaning that arises out of the experience of the absence of meaning should not simply be dismissed by Christian theology as an idolatrous question.[6] Certainly, theology must criticize the widespread tendency to reduce meaning to human action as self-destructive.[7] It is also correct that meaning and truth are not the same.[8] Seductive images may be

---

6. See Gerhard Sauter, *Was heisst nach Sinn fragen? Eine theologisch-philosophische Orientierung* (Munich: C. Kaiser, 1982), pp. 145, 163.

7. Ibid., pp. 39ff., 46ff., 56ff., 130-31.

8. Ibid., pp. 61-62, 88.

experienced as most meaningful—that is the key to their seductiveness, since only for this reason can they lead astray.

Attention to the suffering of meaninglessness can create the false impression that the problem might be solved simply by providing humans with some sort of sense that life is meaningful, as if the content were a peripheral matter and the question of the truth or falsity superfluous and disruptive.[9] Yet if we were to approach the question of meaning that arises out of the experience of meaninglessness as if it were merely a demand to anesthetize nihilistic experience, we would have misunderstood it. Those who earnestly inquire into meaning are concerned with an adequate answer to the problems which have led to the forfeiture of the consciousness of meaning.

Thus the question of meaning, correctly understood, is inseparable from the question of truth. This is evidenced by the longing for an all-encompassing meaning. For to the concept of truth belongs the unity of all truth, that is, the simultaneous existence, without contradiction, of each individual truth with all other truths. From this insight alone it should be clear that the question of the meaning-context of reality as a whole is not theologically illegitimate.[10] To inquire into the total meaning of reality is not automatically an expression of human presumptuousness. It is a matter of fact that the individual is everywhere conditioned by the whole, and the consciousness of this state of affairs belongs essentially to what it means to be human. To be sure, the simul-

---

9. For a critique of this position, see ibid., pp. 105, 107-8.

10. Sauter comes at least very close to such a thesis, inasmuch as he flatly characterizes the meaning question (as a question concerning absolute meaning) as "immoderate and presumptuous" (ibid., p. 167). He brings the alleged avoidance of this question by Job and Kohelet (Ecclesiastes) into connection with the Old Testament prohibitions of images of God. Nevertheless, Sauter also says that the question of meaning belongs to life itself (pp. 128-29), and speaks of the "meaning that is communicated in the cross of Christ" (pp. 152ff.).

taneous awareness that we can never gain a definitive over-view of the whole of reality is also a part of our humanity. Only when this is forgotten is it appropriate to speak of presumptuousness.

Knowledge about the whole of reality itself and the question of its basis must not be confused with this sort of presumptuousness. The presumption lies in alleging to com-mand a definitive view over the whole, whereby persons forget their own finitude and place themselves in the position of God. In contrast, the sort of knowledge of the whole of reality that remains conscious at the same time of its own finiteness reaches consummation in a knowledge of God as distinct from human subjectivity. The idea of God as such is always an answer to the question of the meaning of reality as a whole. Whoever wishes to exclude this question must also forbid that religious consciousness through which we honor God as the creator of ourselves and the world.

It is certainly appropriate to a correct knowledge of God that we include an allusion to divine inscrutability. Yet this allusion must not be understood as an attempt to avoid an-swering the question of the meaning-context of reality as a whole. Instead, it represents a phase in such an answer, insofar as it emphasizes the superiority of the God-based meaning of the life-world as a whole over and above the limitations of human understanding. Even negative theology, which refuses to go beyond the conception of the unknown God, is in this sense an answer to the human question of meaning. Of course, it is not the Christian answer, for Christianity confesses that in Jesus of Nazareth the divine Logos has become human, the one in whom all things have their being. The Greek word *logos* connotes "meaning" as much as "word." The connection of the Old Testament concept of the divine Word with the Greek notion of *logos* means nothing less than that the context of meaning which encompasses the entire creation and its his-tory up through the eschatological completion has been made manifest in Jesus Christ.